MAN
EDUCATION
AND WORK

MAN
EDUCATION
AND WORK
POSTSECONDARY VOCATIONAL AND TECHNICAL EDUCATION

by Grant Venn

assisted by
Theodore J. Marchese, Jr.

AMERICAN COUNCIL ON EDUCATION
WASHINGTON, D.C.

Foreword

VOCATIONAL AND TECHNICAL EDUCATION have recently assumed a new importance in this country. The dramatic rise in youth unemployment and underemployment, the shortage of badly needed personnel in many technical, semiprofessional, and skilled occupations, the retraining and continuing education needs of workers displaced by automation, and the rising demand for new educational opportunities both at the secondary and postsecondary levels have forced a re-examination of this nation's long-standing neglect of occupational education.

Passage of the Vocational Education Act of 1963 was one outcome of that re-examination. Its provisions assure adequate funds for the necessary expansion that lies ahead. But more occupational education does not necessarily mean better occupational education, and one is as important as the other. In presenting this study of postsecondary vocational and technical education, the American Council on Education hopes to improve the climate of public and educational understanding of this field, a climate in which both the availability and adaptability of vocational and technical education can find new growth.

The study which produced this report grew out of a conference called by the American Vocational Association in Washington in September 1962. At that conference representatives of a wide range of interests in vocational and technical education met to discuss possible accreditation of their various programs. It was the consensus of that meeting that before accreditation could proceed on any large scale, some assessment of the place of occupational education within education as a whole and within a new technological economy would have to be made, and that this assessment should be sponsored by the American Council on Education. The Council willingly accepted this task, and during the whole of 1963 a study was conducted under the aegis of its Commission on Academic Affairs.

Dr. Grant Venn, author of the report, was at one time a vocational

v

agriculture instructor in his home state of Washington. He has since served on the education faculty of Washington State University, as superintendent of schools for Othello, Washington, and Corning, New York, as president of Western State College of Colorado, and as director of the Peace Corps training center in Puerto Rico. Since completing his report Dr. Venn has returned to public school administration as superintendent of schools for Wood County (Parkersburg), West Virginia. Theodore J. Marchese, Jr., who assisted Dr. Venn in a research and editorial capacity, is a graduate of Rutgers University; he has served previously on the staffs of Senator Clifford P. Case and the Peace Corps, and is now a staff assistant with the Council. Lawrence E. Dennis, director of the Commission on Academic Affairs, provided editorial supervision for the study.

While conducting the study, Dr. Venn was assisted by a special advisory committee, consisting of:

Julio B. Bortolazzo, president, College of San Mateo

Shirley Cooper, associate secretary, American Association of School Administrators

Norman C. Harris, associate professor of technical education, Center for the Study of Higher Education, University of Michigan

Kenneth Holderman, coordinator of Commonwealth Campuses, Pennsylvania State University

S. V. Martorana, director, Office of Planning for Higher Education, the State University of New York, New York State Department of Education; *Chairman*

M. D. Mobley, executive secretary, American Vocational Association

Joseph T. Nerden, chief, Division of Vocational Education, Connecticut State Department of Education

Roderick O'Connor, professor of industrial management, Georgia Institute of Technology

Maurice W. Roney, director, School of Industrial Education, Oklahoma State University

Ralph W. Tyler, director, Center for Advanced Study in the Behavioral Sciences

John P. Walsh, deputy director, Office of Manpower, Automation, and Training, U.S. Department of Labor

The Council gratefully acknowledges their assistance. It should be noted that the views expressed in this publication are those of the author and are not necessarily those of either the advisory committee or of any individual committee member. I know, however, that they share the Council's pleasure in bringing this valuable work to fruition.

LOGAN WILSON, *President*
American Council on Education

Contents

List of Tables

1. Man, Education, and Work

TECHNOLOGICAL CHANGE HAS, rather suddenly, thrown up a dramatic challenge to this nation's political, economic, social, and educational institutions. Though the full scope of this challenge may not be comprehended for years to come, its dimensions are now clear enough to call for a massive response on the part of American education. All levels of education, *and particularly postsecondary education,* must quickly move to assume greater responsibilities for preparing men and women for entry into the changed and changing world of technological work. Unless far more and far better education on the semiprofessional, technical, and skilled levels is soon made available to greater numbers of citizens, the national economy and social structure will suffer irreparable damage.

THE PROBLEM

It is the thesis of this report that technology has created a new relationship between man, his education, and his work, in which education is placed squarely between man and his work. Although this relationship has traditionally held for *some* men and *some* work (on the professional level, for example), modern technology has advanced to the point where the relationship may now be said to exist for *all* men and for *all* work. Yet, though technology today in effect dictates the role that education must play in preparing man for work, no level of American education has fully recognized this fact of life. Tragically, the nation's educational system is, when viewed as a whole, in what Edward Chase describes as a gross imbalance, its attention concentrated on the 20 percent of students who go through college.[1] Thus, when Sputnik, one symbol of technological advance, flashed before the world's eyes, the U.S. response was predictable: the National Defense Education Act, designed primarily to bolster science, language, mathematics, and engineering opportunities for the academically talented, degree-seeking student.

[1] Chase, "Learning To Be Unemployable," *Harper's Magazine,* April 1963, p. 33.

1

But what about the other 80 percent who will not graduate from college? Unfortunately, the "pursuit of excellence" has left most of them behind. At the junior high school, high school, and junior college levels, most students, whatever their abilities, aptitudes, and interests, study those subjects that form the high road to the baccalaureate degree. More than a few of them have difficulty appreciating the logic of this course. Despite propaganda about the importance of staying in school, they drift out of educational institutions in droves: the system loses 35 percent of its enrollees during high school, then 45 percent of its high school graduates, and finally 40 percent of its college entrants. Some of this attrition is unavoidable, of course, but, still, large numbers of these dropouts are simply early leavers who are capable of considerably more education than they received. "Lack of interest" is by far the most frequent reason they give for leaving, because they do not fit into the present college-track plan of education. Labor Secretary Willard Wirtz more aptly calls them "push-outs."

And what happens to them when they leave? Turned out of an educational system oriented toward someone else's college degree rather than their own work needs, and entering a labor market whose jobs require constantly higher levels of education and skill development, their prospects are bleak. Fully a fifth of the out-of-school youth under twenty-one are unemployed, and the youth unemployment rate, already higher than it was during the depression, reaches higher levels month after month. Those who do find work end up in low-skill, low-pay jobs, jobs without security and without a future, jobs frustratingly below their occupational potential. Industry has little place for the young worker without a skill; the Armed Forces offer fewer and fewer opportunities for him. At the same time, with two or three years of occupationally oriented education at the high school or junior college level, a great many of these same people could qualify for meaningful jobs on the skilled, technical, and semiprofessional levels, where there are acute manpower shortages. That so many of today's youth did *not* receive adequate occupational education attests a serious shortcoming of the educational system.

The case for greater occupational orientation can be made in terms of this or that number of trained persons needed in certain technical occupations or of employment opportunities needed for the million or more youth not in school and not at work. Important as manpower and jobs are, however, they represent only the opening wedge of the economic and social dislocations the new technology is forcing upon us. To understand the problem more fully, we must look behind these symptoms and examine the new technology and the nature of the changes it has wrought in the relationship between man, his education, and his work.

THE NEW TECHNOLOGY

No one has yet given an adequate definition of "the new technology." Perhaps by nature it is not susceptible of definition. The term is used here to describe the changes now besetting the social and economic institutions of the industrial nations of the world. The emergence of a youth unemployment problem in this country is but one phenomenon indicating the impact of this new technology, an impact which Chase promises will be "impersonal, nonideological, relentless, and possibly overwhelming." [2]

The most significant aspect of the new technology is described by the word *change*. It is not simply a case of new sets of social and economical relationships replacing older ones, but of the new ones themselves being replaced at a faster and faster rate, with only those adapted to change surviving. This concept of change is not new; what *is* new is the *change in the rate of change*. This has come as a result of the tremendous increase in the rate of scientific activity; significantly, the *rate* of that increase is not constant, but *exponential*. One illustration is the Federal expenditure for research and development: it took nine years to double the 1944 expenditure, six years to double the 1953 expenditure, three to double the 1959 expenditure; in 1963 the Federal Government alone spent $14 billion on research and development, ten times the amount spent for that purpose only a dozen years ago. This money is fed to a growing army of scientific, engineering, and technical personnel, who have, according to a Stanford Research Institute report to the United States Senate, "invented the art of systematic invention." The traditional tools of the "art" have been vastly augmented by the development of data processing, linear programing, systems analysis, and simulation. The "decision theorists" of the new technology now seek, in the words of economist Daniel Bell, "the compass of rationality itself."

[2] Edward Chase, "Politics and Technology," *Yale Review,* March 1963, p. 321.

Many theorists of the new technology have contemplated whether all this represents a revolution comparable to the industrial revolution begun two centuries ago. Perhaps it is too early to answer that question; as John Diebold put it, this is "an extremely complex subject—we are long on conjecture and short on all but the most basic facts." [3] But by considering the changes already brought about by the new technology, its potential for new change, and the rate at which change is occurring, it is possible to accept Donald Michael's thesis that the new technology is something "so different in degree as to be a profound difference in kind." [4]

The landmark of technological developments has been the introduction of automation and computers into industry and commerce. *Automation* encompasses a class of devices that automatically perform both the sensing and the motor tasks formerly performed by human labor. Thus, automated machines can mine coal, pick cotton, cast and finish engine blocks, sort bank checks, roll aluminum, grade oranges, and weave cloth. *Computers* are devices which rapidly perform traditional human tasks involving experience, memory, analysis, logic, and decision-making. Such devices now can diagnose symptoms for the physician, research a case for the lawyer, read envelopes for the postman, analyze market portfolios for the broker, design a plant for the architect, prepare war and defense plans for the military, fly missiles for the scientist, screen volunteers for the Peace Corps, and keep inventory for the merchant. These machines are being "taught" to translate languages, compose music, play chess, transcribe speech, and "see" objects; already they correct their mistakes and identify trouble spots in their mechanism.

The impact of these devices on the labor market has been profound. Automatic elevators have recently displaced 40,000 elevator operators in New York City alone. New equipment in the Census Bureau enabled 50 statisticians to do the work in 1960 that required 4,000 such people in 1950. The check-writing staff in the Treasury Department has been reduced from 400 people to four. The airline flight engineer and the railroad fireman may soon disappear completely. Ponderous mechanical cotton pickers have, in the last four years, reduced farm jobs in lush

[3] Diebold, Governor's Conference on Automation, State of New York, June 1–3, 1960.

[4] Michael, *Cybernation: The Silent Conquest* (Santa Barbara, Calif.: Center for the Study of Democratic Institutions, 1962), p. 5.

Tulare County, California, from 25,000 to 17,000. Thirty thousand packinghouse workers have been "automated out" of their jobs in the past few years. Enormous machines have helped reduce employment in the coal fields from 415,000 in 1950 to 136,000 in 1962. While construction work has leaped 32 percent since 1956, construction jobs have shown a 24 percent decline. Comparable statistics exist for the chemical, aircraft, communications, metals, transportation, and other industries. In many additional cases where automation and computers have been introduced, the effect has not yet been to fire or lay off, but rather to put a moratorium, or freeze, on new hiring.

Assuredly this is only the beginning; a steady increase in job dislocation can be predicted as the nation accelerates into what Daniel Bell labels a "postindustrial society." Domestic and international competition compel greater reliance on the speed and precision possible only with these devices. In turn, they are being designed to do larger and larger portions of the tasks now performed by human labor at the same time that they are becoming less expensive in relation to the costs of human labor. It seems only a matter of time until a substantial part of the present national employment succumbs to technological advance; many of the present tasks of farm workers, laborers, semiskilled operatives, service workers, craftsmen, and middle management administrators have a high likelihood of technological elimination.

The full impact of the new technology has been slow to register on the American consciousness. To date, the instances of "technological unemployment" are like the cap of an iceberg: the difficulty of appreciating what is below lures many into believing we can sail blithely ahead without changing course. Indeed, the nation has been assured for years that for every job destroyed by automation two new ones are created, and this notion has been slow to die. Because automation and computers have been introduced selectively, their impact has often been limited to the individual or a local community. Thus, many educators and other public leaders have not discerned that the forces of technology are *immediate* in importance and *national* in scope, and that they carry serious consequences for the economic and social life of the entire country.

The nation's task is to make certain that the human promise of America is not lost to the economic promise of technology. In this decade the issue is joined: young people are entering a technological world of work unequipped with the tools they need for survival. More than a million of them are now out of school and out of work and, given the circumstances, this figure can but continue to rise. The alternatives before the country are clear:

We can try to hold young people in school and off the labor market for a longer period of time, by simply expanding the educational system.

We can let them remain idle.

We can put them to work "raking leaves from the public lawn."

We can equip them in school and in college with the skills they need to become competitive in a technological work world.

But as of now, James B. Conant warns us, "unemployment of youth is literally nobody's affair."

This report is primarily concerned with the impact of technology on American education. The measure of impact is best described by the far-reaching changes induced by technological advance in the relationship between man, his education, and his work.

MAN AND WORK

The past few decades have seen many changes in the American work world. Child labor has disappeared; the arrival of the forty-hour (or less) workweek means that people do less work; the use of machines (and of machines to control machines) means that what work remains is physically less demanding. But these obvious changes obscure more fundamental alterations in the world of work that have significance for man and his education.

Work becoming more cognitive. The industrial revolution greatly affected the way in which people worked. As animal and human muscle power were replaced by steam and electric power, the blue-collar operative and the skilled tradesman became the dominant figures in an economy based on industrial production. Now the advent of the new technology has led us into a further stage of work activity in which the emphasis on manipulative powers has shifted to emphasis on the cognitive powers. Lee A. DuBridge has described how technology has changed the industrial production processes in terms of

. . . the multiplicity of electronic devices now used to control industrial processes—to monitor the quality of the product and adjust the machine to correct for deviations, to compute in advance the rate at which materials and parts of particular types should be fed into a complex assembly line, and to continue the process of taking over more and more of the repetitious processes formerly done by hand—and performing them with a delicacy, precision, and speed that human hands could never match.[5]

Automation, then, supplants human manipulation and control of machines with electronic control devices, replacing machine operators with a supervisor of the automatically controlled operating system. In the automated office, high-speed computers and data-processing equipment have necessitated revamping the procedures and the job descriptions for such processes as auditing, bookkeeping, account-keeping, payroll, and inventory. Employers in both plant and office look for people with higher levels of education and more sophisticated skills to perform the more cognitive work functions involved.[6]

The shift from manual to cognitive work is reflected in the long-term changes in the occupational distribution of the labor force, shown in Table 1. In 1900 the number of white-collar jobs was less than half the number of blue-collar jobs, whereas by 1975 it is projected to be almost 44 percent greater. Equally important, semiskilled operatives, traditionally the backbone of the industrial (and manual) work force, have reached their highest proportion and begun to decline. Within the blue-collar and white-collar groups similar trends are apparent. Within the blue-collar ranks, only the skilled and highly skilled craftsmen are expected to maintain their proportion in the labor market, and in recent years the biggest employment gains within the white-collar area have

---

[5] DuBridge, "Educational and Social Consequences," in *Automation and Technological Change,* ed. John T. Dunlop (Englewood Cliffs, N.J.: Prentice-Hall, 1962), p. 30.

[6] Yale economist Neil Chamberlain, in a paper on "Automation and Labor Relations" delivered at Reed College, Nov. 17, 1961, cited a Bureau of Labor Statistics study of the effect of electronic data-processing equipment installations on office personnel. "In offices where the new equipment was introduced, 17 percent of the original work force had not completed high school. After the new equipment had been installed, among those retained, the number of high school nongraduates decreased to 5 percent. Among new hires for positions in these installations, there are only 1 percent who have not reached this educational level. In the same operations, only 7 percent of the original group of employees had completed four years or more of college, as against 42 percent of those retained for the new installation, and 78 percent of those being newly hired."

been made by the most highly educated and skilled group (professional and technical workers). These shifts are indicative that white-collar jobs will continue to encroach into all sectors of the labor force and that, excepting service workers, the occupations that will grow the most are those demanding higher levels of education and skill development.

TABLE 1

Major Occupational Groups as a Percentage of Total Labor Force, Representative Years

Occupational Group	1900*	1947†	1960‡	1975‡
White-collar workers	*17.6*	*34.9*	*43.1*	*47.8*
Professional and technical	4.3	6.6	11.2	14.2
Managers and proprietors	5.8	10.0	10.6	10.7
Clerical workers	3.0	12.4	14.7	16.2
Sales personnel	4.5	5.9	6.6	6.7
Blue-collar workers	*35.8*	*40.7*	*36.3*	*33.4*
Craftsmen and foremen	10.5	13.4	12.8	12.8
Semiskilled operatives	12.8	21.2	18.0	16.3
Laborers (exclusive of farm and mine)	12.5	6.1	5.5	4.3
Service workers	*9.0*	*10.4*	*12.5*	*14.3*
Farm workers	*37.6*	*14.0*	*8.1*	*4.5*

* Computed from U.S. Bureau of the Census, *Historical Statistics of the United States, Colonial Times to 1957* (Washington: Government Printing Office, 1960), pp. 75–78.
† *Manpower Report of the President and A Report on Manpower Requirements, Resources, Utilization, and Training by the United States Department of Labor, Transmitted to the Congress, March 1963* (Washington: Government Printing Office, 1963), p. 143.
‡ *Ibid.*, p. 100. Figures for 1975 are projected.

In the past increases in white-collar employment came from the expansion of jobs in teaching, banking, government, insurance, and the like. But in recent years a considerable portion of the increase has come from *within* industry. Between 1948 and 1960, for example, the number of blue-collar production workers *declined* by nearly a half-million, while nonproduction white-collar workers rose 1.5 million. In large corporations such as General Motors, United States Steel, Du Pont, and Standard Oil, over 35 percent of all employees are now white-collar. The magnitude of this shift, essentially from manual to mental work, can be seen in Table 2.

Industries in the so-called primary sector of the economy, largely agriculture and mining, which in the past have employed large numbers of unskilled workers, have undergone drastic reductions in numbers of jobs in recent years: counting production workers only, mining and agricultural employment has decreased about 40 percent in the last fifteen years. In industry, the secondary sector, production and over-all employment have gained, but employment of laborers and semiskilled operatives has shown *no increase at all*. Employment opportunities in the lower reaches of the spectrum—the jobs that require lesser amounts of education and skill development—have become severely limited. Yet these jobs are the traditional entry point for most young workers. The contemporary technological economy has little to offer the untrained, undereducated would-be worker. There is no room at the bottom.

TABLE 2

Ratio of Nonproduction Worker Employment to Total Employment, Selected Industries, 1947 and 1962**

Industry Group	1947	1962
Ordnance	18.5	54.0
Instruments	20.2	36.3
Petroleum	23.1	35.7
Transportation equipment	18.5	31.8
Machinery	20.9	30.4

* *Manpower Report of the President and A Report on Manpower Requirements, Resources, Utilization, and Training by the United States Department of Labor, Transmitted to the Congress, March 1963*, p. 165. "Nonproduction workers" include people in personnel, administration, marketing, research, and the like.

Occupation and status.   As technology changes the world of work, it inevitably affects the relationship between man and his work. The crucial factor is the importance of the job itself to the individual in American society. Without an occupational status, Brookover and Nosow remind us, "the individual has few other statuses which are capable of offering him a respected position in the community." [7]

This was not always so. Before the Civil War, for example, the

[7] Wilbur B. Brookover and Sigmund Nosow, "A Sociological Analysis of Vocational Education in the United States," *Education for a Changing World of Work: Report of the Panel of Consultants on Vocational Education*, Appendix III (Washington: Government Printing Office, 1963), p. 26.

national economy was centered on the primary industries—agriculture, mining, forestry, fishing, construction, transportation, and the like. The function of work in that economy was the production of goods, such as food, clothing, shelter, and raw materials. The prime instruments of production were human and animal strength, and the very inefficiency of these instruments meant that production could never be much above subsistence levels; it took four families on the farm to feed one in the city. The economist labels this condition "scarcity."

In such a setting "work" was defined in terms of physical effort. A man's status was determined, not by the job he held, but by the amount of work he could do, by the amount of goods he could produce through physical effort. Americans heard the same message from the pulpit: the Puritan work ethic taught that hard work was necessary to salvation; idle hands were the devil's helper. The lone exception was the "gentleman"; whatever his occupation, what he did was not classified as work.

Today the forces of industrialism and technology have altered the meaning of the word "work" and man's relation to the world of work. The displacement of muscle power by the automated machine makes possible the production of vast surpluses of goods; abundance has replaced scarcity.

The blue-collar–white-collar shift in the employment force signifies that the primary function of work in our economy today is to secure, not the production of goods, but their distribution. In 1900, for example, 70 percent of the nation's labor force was engaged in production, compared with less than 40 percent today. And only a very small percentage of the present labor force is engaged in what earlier centuries would call "hard work."

This situation leads to the problem at hand. As Gerard Piel points out, any hard work that a machine can do (and that includes virtually all such work) is better done by a machine; "hard" these days means mostly boring and repetitive, whether in the factory or the office. But the instinct for workmanship, the need to feel needed, the will to achieve, are deeply felt in every human heart. "They are not," says Piel, "universally fulfilled by the kind of employment most people find." [8] Indeed, with the enactment of social legislation such as workman's

[8] Piel, *Consumers of Abundance* (Santa Barbara, Calif.: Center for the Study of Democratic Institutions, 1961), p. 9.

compensation and unemployment relief and with the steady downgrading of the manual occupations within our societal values, work itself is no longer an absolute necessity for subsistence or a means of gaining status. *In the place of work we have substituted the job.* A man's occupation in American society is now his single most significant status-conferring role. Whether it be high or low, a job status allows the individual to form some stable conception of himself and his position in the community.[9]

The social and psychological effects of joblessness are painfully apparent in America today. They can be seen in the faces of those citizens standing in line for relief checks; none of them may be starving, and there may be work around the home that could keep them busy, but without a job they are lost. Tens of thousands of jobless youth cast about at loose ends, with 80 to 90 percent of the juvenile cases in the courts coming from their ranks. Job discrimination creates a hard knot of frustration in the Negro, frustration that explodes in bitter racial conflict. In this picture should also be noted the woman in her forties, her children grown up, going out to get a job: there still may be plenty of work around the home and the family may not need the money, but she feels a need for new identifications found only in holding a job. This crucial importance of the job to the individual in American society must be borne in mind in a discussion of man, his work, and his education. Statistical compilations of the effect of technology on the labor market can be compelling, but for millions of Americans the problem of joblessness is real and personal.

Youth without jobs. Important as a job may be to his parent, it is no less important to the young person leaving school. For him it is initiation into the adult world. Here again is change, for although the psychological and social significance of the initiation of youth into adulthood has been recognized by every society, it seldom has involved getting a job. In primitive societies initiation often took the form of a prolonged, formal test of physical endurance. Knighting and the sacrament of confirmation performed a similar function in medieval society. In more recent times, American youngsters looked upon shoes or their first pair of long pants as a symbol of adulthood. Some girls had a

---

[9] Brookover and Nosow, "A Sociological Analysis of Vocational Education in the United States," p. 26.

formal coming-out to mark their adulthood; for most girls, marriage was the turning point. But *not* work. Work was something they experienced long before adulthood, whether in the form of helping on the farm or being put into a factory at the age of ten. Since a child has certain physical and manipulative capacities, these were not left idle when the family subsistence depended upon these resources.

But modern society increasingly denies opportunities for work during youth. There are no fires to build, wood to chop, or cows to milk for most young boys and girls; a boy may mow the lawn or wash the car, a girl may vacuum the rugs or wash dishes, but little formal work awaits them until they get a job. Since the modern economy hires only more mature people, and since adults themselves measure status in terms of jobs, a job becomes the symbol of acceptance into the adult world. Neither religious ceremonies (which come too early), nor marriage (which for many comes too late), nor school graduation ceremonies (a good excuse for some new clothes and a round of parties) rank even close to the job as an initiation symbol.

This is not to suggest that something is wrong with the value system of American youth. These are simply the values of the adult world, and every young person has always looked forward to being an adult and doing the things adults do. Today, this means getting a job, the assumption of an occupational status. The big difficulty is that when young men and women leave school, they find there is no ready transition into the world of work. There are no jobs for them. The consequences of this, Dr. Conant tells us, represent "social dynamite."

There are now more than *one million* young men and women under twenty-two who have left school and are not at work. At any given time 30 percent of the high school dropouts will be unemployed; even high school graduates average 15 percent unemployed. The figure for college dropouts is considerably lower, but they share the same problem as those who have dropped out of the system earlier: there is little room in the labor market for the undereducated, unskilled young worker. Instead of initiation they find rejection.

The consequences are enormous. The alarmingly high incidence of delinquency and crime among jobless youth is well documented; less widely appreciated is the tremendous reservoir of idleness, frustration, resentment, and defeat that lies within their burgeoning numbers. Lacking jobs, "their badge of belonging," reports the President's Committee on Youth Employment, these young men and women represent "tomorrow's castoffs and chronic dependents, those who will live in poverty of body and mind, and who will bring up their children in their own image." [10]

Youth with jobs. Public discussion of the problems of youth and work has generally focused on the plight of the high school dropout who cannot find a job. Of equal concern should be the worsening of another important problem—youth *under*employment.

A job is vital to the young person, and it is also vital that the job provide an outlet for his abilities, that it be compatible with his considered aspirations. These conditions are seldom met in the entry jobs now available to young men and women with limited education and skills. When they *are* able to find a job, typically they enter the labor market at a very low level. The high school dropout may find a job washing dishes or parking cars; if he has graduated from high school or attended college awhile, he may clerk in a store or become a route salesman. These are dead-end jobs, and he knows it. He becomes frustrated; initiation for him has become a personal defeat. Chances are he will soon quit his job and seek another; job turnover among people under twenty-two is far higher than among older workers and is more happenstance than planned. At the Los Angeles Trade-Technical College the average student (now in his twenties) has gone through an average of ten jobs before coming to Trade-Tech. "They have been defeated," says Dean of Instruction Franklin R. Johnson. "You can see defeat in their eyes." [11]

Some people believe that the solution to the problem of youth and work lies simply in keeping all students in school at least through high school graduation. Many college administrators, who watch 40 percent of their entering freshmen drop out along the way, act as though the whole problem was far removed from their province, that any time spent in college is to the good. Their assumption seems to be that the best and only necessary preparation for a job today is the longest possible immersion in academic and professional subjects.

[10] President's Committee on Youth Employment, *The Challenge of Jobless Youth* (Washington: Government Printing Office, 1963), p. iv.
[11] Quoted by George B. Leonard, "Are We Cheating Twenty Million Students?", *Look*, June 4, 1963, p. 38.

This assumption at once fails to heed the factor of youth unemployment and misapprehends the relevance of general education. The liberal, or academic, studies *do* enhance the long-range civic and occupational competence of a person; they *do not,* at least below the baccalaureate degree level and as a rule, qualify young people for meaningful job entry. The technological work world is one of specialization and sophisticated skills, and being a "bright young man" cuts relatively little ice with employers looking for skills to do some specific kind of work. A review of the help wanted section of any newspaper confirms this. Norman C. Harris says:

> The fact is that although business and industry would like to have employees with a higher level of general education and a concomitant higher potential for subsequent promotion, for *entry jobs* in the American economy today competence and skill of a rather high order, in some facet of the world of work are absolutely essential.[12]

When the dropouts from the four-year colleges and graduates of junior college academic programs do not find meaningful entry jobs, they experience *under*employment rather than unemployment, and the underemployment of those with some college study heightens *un*employment among those with no college work. The young man with a year or two of college working at the supermarket check-out counter may well have the ability to be a highly skilled craftsman or technician. By taking a job at the supermarket, he creates a double loss in our manpower pool: the job at the higher ability level remains vacant while he displaces the lower-ability person who could function well in that position.

Job selection in the technological work world has become a desperate affair, often subject to wildest chance and equally often unrelated to the young job seeker's aptitudes and abilities. Many young people are unaware of the range of occupations and have had little opportunity to observe work in its setting. A century ago the young boy or girl participated in the work of the family and had a good idea of what the other men and women of the community did. Today they may know what the home repairman, policeman, shopkeeper, and the truckdriver do, but understand little about the work of the chemist, the electrician, the

[12] Harris, "Meeting the Post-High School Educational Needs of the Vast 'Middle Group' of High School Graduates," Presentation to the North Central Association of Colleges and Secondary Schools, Committee on Articulation of Schools and Colleges, Chicago, March 19, 1963, p. 3.

lathe operator, or the construction worker. Thus intelligent transition into the world of work becomes all the more difficult and vocational guidance all the more essential.

WORK AND EDUCATION

The institutions of the technological society are intellectual ones, and the use of cognitive faculties becomes paramount in work, as it has always been in education. Over a wide range of occupations in the new technology, job entry and upgrading become increasingly a matter of education; more of what is basic to successful performance in today's occupations can best be taught within formal educational frameworks.

Occupation linked to education. The relationship between educational achievement and occupational entry and upgrading is demonstrated by the median years of schooling of workers within the major occupational groups, shown in Table 3. The educational level of persons within these different occupations tells the same story, shown in Table 4.

TABLE 3

*Median Years of School Completed as of
March 1962, by Major Occupational Group**

Occupational Group	*Median Years of Schooling*
White-collar workers	
Professional and technical	16.2
Managers and proprietors	12.5
Clerical workers	12.5
Sales personnel	12.5
Blue-collar workers	
Craftsmen and foremen	11.2
Semiskilled operatives	10.1
Laborers (exclusive of farm and mine)	8.9
Other	
Service workers	10.8
Farm workers	8.6

* *Manpower Report of the President and A Report on Manpower Requirements, Resources, Utilization, and Training by the United States Department of Labor, Transmitted to the Congress, March 1963, p. 13.*

These tables summarize the educational attainment of those already in the labor force, many of whom entered years ago under circumstances quite different from those prevailing now.

TABLE 4

*Levels of Educational Attainment within Major
Occupational Groups, by Percentage**

| | PERCENT WITH | | |
OCCUPATIONAL GROUP	Less Than High School Diploma	High School Diploma Only	Some College Education
Professional and technical................	6	19	75
Proprietors and managers.................	38	33	29
Clerical and sales workers................	25	53	22
Skilled workers.........................	59	33	8
Semiskilled workers.....................	70	26	4
Service workers.........................	69	25	4
Unskilled workers.......................	80	17	3
Farmers and farm managers..............	76	19	5

* U.S. Department of Labor, *Manpower, Challenge of the 1960's* (Washington: Government Printing Office, 1961), p. 17.

The tables do not tell the full story of the educational requisites for young people entering an occupation today. A high school diploma is a minimum requisite for most production workers, and a bachelor's degree, often in engineering, may be a requisite for the foreman or supervisor. A college education is the only ticket for entry into the professions, with graduate study often a necessity for advancement. The technical, skilled, and semiprofessional occupations all demand substantial amounts of postsecondary education for entrance. In the accelerating job-upgrading process of technology there is a steady increase of higher education and skills needed for entry and retention. Education has become the crucial ladder to the reward positions in society. Of the undereducated and untrained, Secretary Wirtz says:

> The reason for the increasing concentration of unemployment among unskilled workers is that machines are taking over the unskilled jobs. These are the jobs which have, up to this time, absorbed the casualties of the educational system: Those who for one reason or another have left school without having added to the strength which is in their arms and backs the skill it takes to do something more than "common labor." This wasn't too bad when there were enough common labor jobs around. Now there aren't.

Today, unskilled workers make up 5 percent of the work force, but almost 15 percent of all the unemployed are in this group. Unemployment is over twice as high among the young worker groups and among non-white workers—the two groups in which there are the largest percentages of unskilled workers—than it is in the work force as a whole.[18]

The relationship between education and work, in terms of occupational entry and upgrading, is fixed and firm.

Broadening the relationship. The link between education and work at the highest occupational levels is well recognized. In the research and development field, for example, the line between education and work is very thin. Both university and industry will take on cost-plus contracts in the same field, and interchange of personnel between the two is frequent. Many of the space research companies are direct university offshoots; over-all, the great bulk of research and development is concentrated geographically around the top universities. The professions, it has long been agreed, are a proper subject of academic attention, and preparation for them should take place within a formal educational framework.

Now, technology has advanced many occupations on the technical, skilled, and semiprofessional levels to a point where they require higher levels of specialization and related knowledge that are best learned and taught within educational frameworks. Manifestations of this upward push are to be found, for example, in engineering, where the two-year engineering technology curricula of today compare in rigor and breadth with the four-year engineering curricula of twenty-five years ago. As engineering continues to become more complex and specialization is delayed, graduate study will become a must for the engineer, and, by the same token, it is probable that within the present decade the bachelor's degree will become a must for many technical occupations. Similarly, the skilled crafts are now making their appearance on the junior college level.

Inevitably, in the same way that pupilage and apprenticeship gave way to professional education in law and medicine, on-the-job training

---

[18] Statement of W. Willard Wirtz before the Subcommittee on Education, Senate Committee on Labor and Public Welfare, on S. 580, "National Education Improvement Act of 1963," April 30, 1963, p. 2.

and apprenticeship are giving way to occupational education within the educational system. The time has come for schools and colleges to recognize that the new occupations of technology must be taught where they are best able to be learned.

MAN AND EDUCATION

At a time when the demand for education, especially higher education, has never been greater, is it *necessary* that vocational and technical occupations be taught within the educational system? In the past, perhaps no; now, however, yes, because technology is demanding workers with a degree of training and related education that can best be offered in a *system* of education. To ignore the demand is to accept social and economic dislocations that will vitally affect the American economy and the personal well-being of our citizens.

The impact of technology. The labor market will be the focal point of these dislocations: as a technological economy expands, the largest increase in jobs will occur in occupations that require the most education and training (see Table 5).

TABLE 5

Percentage Change in Employment, by Major Occupational Groups, 1960-75*

Occupational Group	Percentage Increase, 1960 to Projected 1975
Professional and technical	65
Managers and proprietors	32
Clerical workers	45
Service workers	51
Sales workers	34
Skilled workers	30
Semiskilled operatives	18
Laborers (exclusive of farm and mine)	—
Farm workers	—28

* *Manpower Report of the President and A Report on Manpower...,* p. 100.

Only a reconciliation of education, the new occupational requirements, and the potential of our people to fill them can prevent labor dislocations—an economy permanently sluggish for lack of the educated and skilled people needed to maintain its momentum, and, at the same time, a large and dangerous body of unemployed and underemployed, too poorly educated and skilled to participate in the new technological economy.

These dislocations have already begun to make their appearance. The most obvious, already cited, is the heavy concentration of unemployment among the poorly educated and the unskilled, where despite the current liveliness in the economy, some 6 percent of American workers cannot find work, including 18 percent of our out-of-school youth.

There are some forecasts that the coming years will be characterized by great economic growth in this country; equally reputable forecasters, however, tell us bluntly that our unemployment rate can be expected to continue its long-term upward climb. Columbia philosopher Charles Frankel has pointed out that as technology continues to loosen the spirit of invention and innovation, not only will we have technological unemployment, "but we can count on it as a *normal feature* and sign that our system is doing well." Although all the consequences of technological innovation cannot be foreseen, we do know that its social and economic effects are dislocating. Therefore, adds Frankel, we should not panic, treating the dislocations as an "accident," as "something that shouldn't happen." What we must do, he concludes, is deliberately establish permanent preventive institutions carefully designed to cope with such dislocations as we can anticipate.[14]

Impact on employment. Unemployment—a dislocation we can anticipate—is in part caused by the technological means for economizing the use of labor outrunning the pace at which new uses for that labor are found. Estimates of the number of workers displaced each year by automation now run in the order of one and a half million. These people become difficult to absorb in a labor market already burdened with unemployment and an increasing number of job-seeking youth.

At the same time that technological unemployment grows, there are, by various rough estimates, some four million unfilled jobs in the country today. Technology, as it destroys jobs, also creates new ones; for example, while elevator operators are losing their jobs to automatic eleva-

[14] Frankel, Remarks at 1961 National Conference on Social Welfare, quoted in Chase, "Politics and Technology," p. 329.

tors, new jobs are created in the design, building, sale, installation, and servicing of the new equipment. But the newly created jobs are not likely to be filled by the displaced workers unless they have the educational potential and training opportunities to meet the requirements of the new jobs. The problem, then, is one of distribution of the labor force, of matching job requirements and the potential of people to meet them.

The presence of persistent, slowly rising unemployment shows that the nation is far from coping with this problem. If the holding of a job is as important to the individual as this report has indicated, then full employment must be a national goal. And in the words of Labor Secretary Willard Wirtz, "full employment in this country depends on full education." [15]

As recently as a year or two ago there existed a general consensus that the problem of persistent unemployment could be solved simply by stepping up the rate of national growth. Now, however, it is increasingly clear that no *attainable* rate of growth can in and of itself solve this nation's employment problems. This shift represents a remarkable shift in contemporary economic thought. The unemployed are the undereducated and underskilled, and in the years ahead economic growth, increasingly a creature of technological advance, will not substantially increase the number of jobs for such people. Preventive measures to meet the dislocations of technological displacement must include the development of new occupational competencies for a major part of the labor force. This task will essentially be an educational one.

Willard Wirtz summarizes this point as follows:

> What this means in terms of educational needs is obvious. We simply cannot any longer afford to let boys and girls leave the educational system unprepared to use their minds as well as their muscles. We must, in one way or another, see to it that they have what today's— and tomorrow's—labor market requires. The margin for educational error or failure, which is what the unskilled jobs in the old work force constituted, has been taken up by the machine.[16]

Economic growth. A second technological dislocation pointing to the necessity for more and better occupational education is economic in nature and involves the worsening shortage of personnel in many skilled, professional, and technical occupations. It will be the personnel in these

---

[15] Wirtz testimony on S. 580, *op. cit.,* p. 1.
[16] *Ibid.,* p. 2.

fields who will be most involved in the work that engenders further technological advance. In this age of the art of systematic invention and innovation, the *rate* of invention and innovation—or more broadly of technological advance—depends to a large extent on the number of technical "artists" available for the tasks at hand. The evidence is that in the decades ahead the rate of economic growth will be increasingly dependent upon the rate of technological development. And since the rate of technological advance depends on the availability of technical personnel, the education of people in the professional, technical, and skilled occupations becomes a prime factor in increasing the growth rate of the national enterprise.[17]

Manpower needs on the professional level, especially for scientists and engineers, are widely known, and need not be discussed here. Suffice it to say that the shortages are acute, and almost certainly will become greater. A considerable amount of effort has been put into improving the situation; more needs to be done.

The need for technical personnel, however, is not so clearly understood, and deserves greater attention immediately. Industry is learning that not only is it faced with shortages of scientists and engineers but that it often is not making full use of the real skills of those it has. Various studies show that many of the routine functions of the scientist and engineer could be performed by people with more limited, specialized training. Thus, in the years ahead we will need many more new technicians than scientists and engineers; for example, while the most desirable ratio of technicians to scientists and engineers is, depending on field and industry, between 2 to 1 and 4 to 1,[18] recent inventories show existing ratios of from .5 to 1 to .9 to 1.[19] In bread-and-

[17] Walter W. Heller, chairman of the President's Council of Economic Advisers, noted recently that "A series of studies for the United States shows that about half of the increase in output over the last fifty years must be attributed to factors other than the increase in the stock of tangible capital and man-hours worked," with "technology and brainpower" inputs accounting for the rest of the growth. Interestingly, most of these "intangible inputs," says Heller, "originate in education and training." (Heller, "Men, Money, and Materials," *Educational Record*, January 1963, pp. 13–14.)

[18] For a discussion, see Lynn A. Emerson, "Technical Training in the United States," *Education for a Changing World of Work: Report of the Panel of Consultants on Vocational Education*, Appendix I (Washington: Government Printing Office, 1963), p. 36.

[19] Bureau of Labor Statistics, *The Long-Range Demand for Scientific and Technical Personnel*, Prepared for the National Science Foundation (Washington: Government Printing Office, 1961), p. 44.

butter terms, this gross misuse of professional manpower can be corrected only through a greatly stepped-up program of technical education, geared to an output of approximately 100,000 graduating technicians a year.[20]

A similar situation prevails in the skilled occupations. An estimated 5.2 million jobs will open up in this area during this decade, all requiring people with highly developed skills and considerable related knowledge. Most of these occupations are in the apprenticeable trades; however, apprenticeship completions will probably number no more than 300,000 to 400,000 during this ten-year period, as this traditional but increasingly unsuitable source of skilled workers continues to decline. This leaves an *annual shortage* in this area of nearly a *half-million skilled craftsmen,* a shortage that will make itself acutely felt in the years ahead. The potential of education to meet the need for skilled workers has been amply demonstrated over the years by the better vocational trades and industry programs on the high school and post-high-school level in several states, and more recently by the ambitious programs of many of the California community colleges. The need for a sustained educational effort in this area is great.

Impact of increase in population. The immediacy of the problem being discussed in this report is underscored by the burgeoning numbers of students now leaving or about to leave the nation's educational system for the world of work.

During the 1950's the number of young workers entering the labor force each year was relatively stable; in 1959 there were only a half-million more of them in the labor force than in 1950. During the present decade, however, the number of young workers seeking to enter the labor force will increase by 6 million. The flood of World War II babies, now completing their education, is about to surge into the world of work; for every three young entrants into the world of work during 1963, there will be five in the years beyond 1965. One can clearly see what is happening: the number seeking job entry is rapidly increasing, the number of traditional entry jobs is not, and the youth employment problem, with all its attendant social and psychological problems discussed earlier, is going from bad to worse. Obviously, this situation

---

[20] This point will be developed in chap. 3.

could develop into one of the most serious social problems this nation has ever encountered.

But it need not. A significant part of the answer lies in providing *more and better occupational education within the educational system.* More young people must be prepared to enter the world of work at the higher occupational levels where there is room for them and where they are urgently needed.

The student potential. At the present time *only one student in ten leaving the educational system without a bachelor's degree has some specific occupational preparation.* This is only a small fraction of the real student potential for occupational preparation within the educational system.

The magnitude of the student potential is illustrated by the large numbers of students leaving school each year and seeking labor market entry, including nearly a million high school dropouts, more than a million non-college-bound high school graduates, and several hundred thousand college dropouts. As a group these represent 75 to 80 percent of all our youth, and the educational preparation and occupational well-being of this group will in large measure determine the course of this nation in the difficult years ahead. As they leave school, they are ambitious, opportunity-seeking, and still idealistic. In the world of work, however, they are likely to be underemployed, if they find employment at all.

At all educational levels, these unprepared school-leavers entering the work world represent a waste of vital talent. Consider the high school dropout. The image of the dropout is of a dull, rebellious young person. Yet study after study has shown no substantial difference in intelligence between the dropout and his age group as a whole; a recently completed study showed, for example, that *two-thirds* of them were in the IQ range of 90 to 109.[21] These are *average* young men and women, with considerable potential for occupational development within the schools. And they are rebellious only in the sense that for most of them the subjects they studied in school were of little interest. Professor Harris declares that "without a doubt the biggest task facing the

[21] Bureau of Labor Statistics, *From School to Work: The Early Employment Experiences in Seven Communities, 1952–1957* (Washington: Government Printing Office, 1961). The sample involved 22,000 students.

American high school today is to make its curriculum meaningful to students. For hundreds of thousands of boys and girls this meaning must be found in subject and curriculums related to the world of work." [22]

Much of the same is true of the high school graduates who do not go on to college. This group, more than a million strong, represents a high-potential force for post-high-school occupational education. As it stands now, they are having many of the same difficulties in the work world encountered by their classmates who had left school before graduation. Fully 15 percent of these graduates are now unemployed, and undoubtedly a high percentage of those who do have jobs are underemployed. Fifty to 60 percent of the people in this group must eventually find employment as middle-level manpower in the technical, semiprofessional, and skilled occupations for which a one- or two-year college-level program of semiprofessional, technical, or vocational education would provide the ideal preparation.

Higher education too contains a considerable student potential for occupational education of less than baccalaureate level. In many states high school graduates can enter college more readily than they can get a job. For most students going on to college this will mean further academic study leading to the bachelor's degree. It is suggested that there are many students in academic programs of higher education for whom the law of diminishing returns has long since taken effect and who would find a fuller realization of their abilities and interests in a shorter term, specialized occupational program beyond the high school. How much a student profits from his educational experience is more important than the number of years he spends in school.

In this diminishing returns category we count a large proportion of the C students in higher education, many of whom drop out, to be sure, but many of whom drift through four years of college without either finding themselves or quite appreciating what college is all about. We also count many college dropouts (40 percent of all entrants) whose experience in higher education would have been more successful had they enrolled in an occupationally oriented program. Similarly, many junior college students enrolled in a college transfer program might be

---

[22] Harris, "Meeting the Post-High School Educational Needs of the Vast 'Middle Group' of High School Graduates," p. 4.

better off in a terminal occupational program; in point of fact only half of the transfer students actually continue their education.

At the tenth-grade, twelfth-grade, and fourteenth-grade levels the problem is essentially the same. The educational system strives to give each student every opportunity to develop his talents to the highest possible level. But the highest possible level is always defined as the highest possible level of academic or formal education. The B or C student in high school whose real aptitude and ability potential is such that he would find it fully expressed as an engineering technician is nonetheless guided into engineering, and when he becomes an engineering dropout statistic holding some low-level job, it is considered a shame but somehow not the responsibility of higher education. Education pays lip service to the importance of providing an educational response for the wide range of student aptitudes, abilities, and interests, but largely limits that response to general or academic studies of varying degrees of rigor. There are many young people to whom such studies offer little of relevance or challenge, but whose motivations toward educational achievement could be renewed in a more practical program of occupational development suited to their real abilities, aptitudes, and interests. The large number of students with average and above average IQ's found in the attrition between the tenth and fourteenth grades (those who most frequently list "lack of interest" as their reason for leaving school) and the significant number of students with promising IQ's who languish along in secondary and higher education with mediocre academic records are testimony that we are providing an inadequate and inappropriate response to the educational needs of many young men and women. The value of rigorous liberal studies for the academically talented and of a sound general education for all should not lead to the conclusion that these are the only worthy educational endeavors or that this is where the responsibility of education ends.

Occupational education holds the promise of the diversity and practicality that the educational system now lacks in its efforts to educate all our young people to their full potential. Indeed, it is no accident that the city with the most extensive program of secondary vocational education (Milwaukee) is the one city that graduates 94 percent of its students from high school, and that the state with the greatest occupational education opportunities beyond the high school (California) has been able to induce so many of its high school graduates to continue their education.

Continuing education.   The nature and rate of technological change militate against the concept of terminal education. As technology upgrades the skill and knowledge requirements of jobs, education can no longer be confined to the traditional twelve, fourteen, or sixteen years of formal schooling. The Department of Labor projects that the average youth of today will probably shift occupations some five times over the next forty years he is in the labor market. A life of continuing occupational adjustment will mean a life of continuing education to meet changed or additional educational requirements.

Here, flexibility becomes a factor in the school's response to the world of work. Within higher education, for example, subjects might be taught for one week or ten weeks, one year or three years, day or evening, in courses not necessarily coinciding with the academic term, nor necessarily taught by a person with three published articles to students working for degree credit. Robert Weber, pointing to the upgrading of skills with each change of occupation, says in summary that "education must become more modular (less dependent on academic time and status) and that man must go through life with the educational umbilical cord uncut." [23]

The education of women.   The education of women for the world of work poses special problems for the years ahead. The need in this area is not the same as that of older workers or youth in general: one does not find substantial numbers of women on the unemployment lists, the social and psychological implications of a woman not working are not so grave, and the shortages of personnel in most of the subprofessional fields in which women traditionally work are not so acute. On the other hand, it can be expected that the movement of middle-aged women from the home to outside employment will continue; projections indicate, for example, that the number of women past forty-five in the labor force will increase by 30 percent during this decade.

Women have traditionally found employment in the clerical, sales,

[23] Weber, "Man and His Environment—1980," Background paper prepared for the annual meeting of the Board of Trustees of the Educational Testing Service, May 7–8, 1963, p. 27.

light manufacturing, and service occupations. But in light manufacturing, employment opportunities will tend to be fewer, as, for example, the long rows of women soldering circuits on the electronics assembly line are replaced by automated circuit printing machines. Many of the jobs in the service fields are too low level for the better-educated women now seeking re-employment; many other service functions are increasingly subject to automation. A similar situation exists in the clerical and sales fields: these jobs too frequently fall below the ability and aspiration levels of women entering the labor force, and, despite Government figures predicting many new job opportunities in these occupations, the matter is increasingly one of doubt,[24] since the automation of many functions in these areas, already known to be possible, has been relatively slow to date. In short, the future of the woman in the world of work may increasingly be subject to the dislocations already apparent among other working groups.

Serious attention must, therefore, be given to the education and employment of women. A significant breakthrough in this regard is certainly called for in the professions, many of which remain male preserves; similarly, the woman college graduate often finds her education is of little avail unless she possesses clerical skills. These employment barriers at the top (plus other factors) continue to keep high-ability women working at low- and middle-level jobs, jobs which could be filled by women with less education and fewer skills. At the same time greater educational and employment opportunities for women must be made available in the technical occupations, many of which are eminently suited to the particular abilities of women.

Cutting across occupational considerations is the need for educational updating, training, and retraining opportunities for women. The pattern of women in their late thirties and early forties re-entering the labor market as their children grow older will certainly continue. Little educational attention has been paid to this potential source of much-needed talent, which, considering its twenty- to twenty-five–year potential for work, should be more carefully developed. Generally this talent is *under*used. Given opportunities, many women, who have already had considerable education, could find job entry on the technical level or

---

[24] See, for example, Donald N. Michael, *Cybernation: The Silent Conquest,* pp. 14–17.

could become the aides, greatly needed, in teaching, health, recreation, and the social services.

The education of Negroes. Almost any of the problems already discussed could be multiplied by a factor of three to arrive at a fair picture of the size of the problems of the Negro worker. The U.S. Department of Labor reports that during 1962 about one out of four nonwhite teen-agers in the labor force was unemployed, compared with about one out of eight white teen-agers. Since 1955, the jobless rate among Negro youth has risen twice as fast as among white. Nonwhite girls have a much higher unemployment rate than any other group in the entire labor force. Only about one-fifth of the young Negro workers with a high school diploma have white-collar jobs; more than one-half of the young white workers have such jobs.[25]

These national averages obscure much uglier situations in many of our large cities. Although a near-total neglect of this problem makes statistical analysis difficult, Cleveland's pioneering *Unemployed Out-of-School Youth Survey* highlights how tragic a situation may exist.[26] This survey of 1,200 youth (ages sixteen to twenty-two, and involving more than 9,000 separate household contacts) in a Negro district revealed that 63 percent of the out-of-school youth were unemployed, a situation undoubtedly duplicated in ghetto sections of other large cities in the United States.

The Negro population occupies an extraordinary disproportion of lower-class jobs. Comparing only nonfarm workers, one of three white workers is classified as unskilled or semiskilled; but three out of four Negro workers are in this category. With jobs at this level shrinking, the employment gaps between whites and nonwhites are bound to become even more pronounced.

Other figures emphasize the gravity of this country's Negro employment problem and underscore the point that, despite gains in social and legal areas, *the Negro is losing ground in the occupational area,* which, over the long run, will be the most important. Bell, in discussing the postindustrial society of the future, says that, with education now the

[25] Office of Manpower, Automation, and Training, U.S. Department of Labor, *Young Workers: Their Special Training Needs* (Washington: Government Printing Office), pp. 9–11.

[26] Cleveland, Ohio: Cleveland Public Schools. pp. 8, 12.

chief means of social mobility, we can sketch a rough picture of the nation thirty years hence by charting the kind and level of education each of the groups is receiving and matching it against future labor force skill requirements: Class lines in the United States will be predominantly color lines.[27]

The present situation and unacceptability of the situation Bell describes demand that much greater efforts be devoted to Negro education and employment. Equal employment opportunities must be made available. The high incidence of school dropout among Negro youth must be cut. Equally important (as this report will contend) is the necessity of providing opportunities for occupational education through the schools and colleges. Outstanding schools in Baltimore, Chicago, Denver, and Los Angeles have shown that the availability of opportunity on the high school, post-high-school, and collegiate levels can go a long way toward bringing the Negro out of the vicious dropout-unemployment cycle.

WHERE DO WE STAND NOW?

This discussion of the immediate need for more and better occupational education ends with a review of America's efforts to date. At this writing the potential impact of the Vocational Education Act of 1963 cannot be assessed. Prior to its passage, however, the achievement was meager.

The Federal-state cooperative program. Since 1917 the principal vehicle of subprofessional occupational education has been a Federal-state cooperative program of vocational and technical education. It has been a high school program until recent amendments channeled some Federal money to the two-year college level. How has this program fared?

Between 1950 and 1960 secondary school attendance in this country increased some 50 percent. During this same period enrollments in the Federal vocational-technical program rose 10.7 percent. On the high school level, only 6 or 7 percent of all students are now enrolled in

[27] Daniel Bell, "The Post-Industrial Society," Background paper prepared for forum discussion, *The Impact of Technological and Social Change* (Multilithed; Boston: Liberty Mutual Insurance Co., June 14, 1962).

full-time pre-employment courses supported by the Federal program. Only some 5 percent of all junior college students are enrolled in the federally supported technical education program. *Only 2 percent of the 12 million full-time high school students in this country are enrolled in the program's vocational trades and industry division.*

And so the figures read. A more complete discussion of the impact of the federally supported vocational and technical education program, and of state, local, and private efforts in this area, is presented in chapters 3 and 4 of this report. In summary, the total program has never been substantial and has steadily been losing ground over the past several years.

Money available. Over the past decade the national expenditure for education has increased by about 170 percent. The increase in Federal, state, and local expenditures for vocational and technical education was 87 percent. Thus, this form of education, never well financed, has been getting a diminishing portion of the national expenditure on education. These figures, taken with those showing the relative decline in enrollments, indicate the neglect to which vocational and technical education has been subject.

The vocational track. Vocational education has a dual purpose: to provide the people it serves with an education *and* to train skilled workers for the labor force. The fact that the program often does *neither* of these things well has compounded its difficulties, so that its present acceptance within industry and education is all too often lukewarm.

Although the major effort in vocational education is conducted within the public education system, its place within that system has never been clearly defined. Administrative regulations tie it to education's standards and practices, but practical considerations force it to look to industry for its curriculum and teachers. Achievement in vocational subjects may be dependent on achievement in academic subjects, but the two are usually taught without reference to each other. Educational doctrine declares that the schools must be responsive to the full range of student interests, aptitudes, and abilities, but often in practice all but the gifted and retarded are herded through the general academic curriculum. In a great many school systems only those students who appear to have no hope at all of getting into college or who are independently determined to study vocational subjects are guided to the vocational school, which is likely to be labeled "of lower quality," partly because of the students it receives and partly because of a perverted definition of *quality*. Although professional and vocational education may share many similar objectives and methods, one is accepted as education and the other is not.

Finally, though the purpose of education is learning, and though the learning process is by no means reserved to the academic subjects, learning outside these subjects, and especially that obtained in vocational subjects, often finds little recognition. Once a student elects a vocational curriculum, he may be foreclosed from continuing his education in another field; credit for his learning in the vocational area will not be given. His alternatives then become to go back for a year or two and take the approved courses, or leave school. In many states, vocational schools have found that the only way to avoid this dilemma is to burden their students with one or two hours of extra class work each day, so that the students obtain the full load of academic subjects insisted upon by the state for graduation and by the colleges for admission. Needless to say, the lengthened school day does not bring students flocking to the doors of the vocational school, particularly when it may mean giving up an after-school job or a chance to take part in an extracurricular activity.

The election of a vocational program, since it is a somewhat suspect form of education and is not the approved form of preparation for further liberal or professional studies, will often severely limit the student's chances of getting into college. For many students a vocational program in high school represents a closed-end track: since this form of education occupies an ambiguous, peripheral position on all educational levels, there is no clear and acknowledged path to specific occupational goals running up through the secondary and collegiate levels. Vocational subjects may be elected at any stage from the tenth grade on, but there is no logical progression from school to school and level to level, leading to a post-high-school or collegiate degree or potential further study.

In short, effort is scattered and students deterred; only when vocational education is accorded a better-defined and accepted place within the educational community will these obstacles be overcome.

First-job preoccupation. It is an open question whether present forms of vocational and technical education are equal to the demands of a changing world of work. As mentioned earlier, swiftly changing job patterns mean that the subprofessional person must look forward to five or six occupational shifts over the next forty years, so that continuing education will increase in importance. In addition, the more cognitive work functions to be performed will demand higher levels of related knowledge and general education, and a new factor, the anticipated shorter workweek, means that more attention will need to be paid to the use of leisure time and to the potential for greater civic participation.

The high degree of specialization found in many present vocational and technical curricula appears to be misguided. High school students in the federally supported vocational trades and industry program, for example, must spend a minimum of 50 percent of their time in shop work alone. In many technical curricula only 10 percent or less of the school time is allotted to general education subjects. Indeed, the difficulty of placing young people in jobs today, with the premium going to the person who can step into the job with the least amount of additional company instructional time, seems to act as an inducement to vocational and technical schools to concentrate on the expertise needed for nearby job openings. These schools pride themselves on how close their shop facilities duplicate real job conditions, and many of them do have excellent first-job placement records for their graduates. But this does *not necessarily* mean that the school has given the graduate the education he may really need. What is called for is more and better occupational education, to be sure, but occupational education on a more general basis—teaching certain basic skills, of course, but also devoting more time to the development of broader technical understanding, of communication and computational abilities, and of an appreciation of civic, cultural, and leisure activities.

This is more easily said than done. The preoccupation of many vocational and technical education programs with first-job placement is in part the result of inadequate understanding between education and industry. Many schools offering these programs simply do not have the academic resources to give their students the related knowledge and general education background they need, nor do teachers and administrators in these related and general disciplines have the interest or inclination to help vocational and technical educators design the special courses that may be needed. At the same time the vocational and technical school perceives that its program must develop broader occupational and civic understanding in its students, the personnel officer at the local plant is asking graduates of the program, "What job in my shop can you do?" and the foreman complains, "This kid fouled up my machines!" on his first day on the job. This points to the need for occupationally oriented schools and business and commercial interests to maintain close and continuing relationships.

An appropriate division of labor is called for between education and industry, with education doing what it can do best (educate more broadly for a life of work and citizenship), and industry doing what it can do best (train for the specific job). Such a relationship already exists in engineering: educators in the various disciplines have paid considerable attention to the improvement of the liberal and related knowledge content of the engineering curriculum, and as engineering education has, in recent years, become more general, industry has accepted the necessity of spending a longer time breaking in the recent graduate. This relationship must be extended to other occupational fields, particularly the technical and semiprofessional. But only with new status and acceptance within both education and industry will this be possible.

National versus local needs. Vexing problems arise in attempts to gear vocational and technical programs to the present and future world of work. On the one hand, the choice among occupational offerings is in the hands of local boards and administrators, who are under pressure to tailor the program to the more immediate manpower needs of local (tax-paying) industry. On the other hand, the industrial complex of the nation is being made and remade so swiftly, and plant and worker mobility are so high that narrow, local training may have short relevance for the new worker. This again points to the importance of a more broadly based vocational-technical education, one consonant with long-term regional and national manpower demands.

Lag. The lag between what is taught in the school and what is actually practiced in industry constitutes a related problem. The school that invests heavily in shop and laboratory equipment in an attempt to duplicate industrial conditions soon learns it cannot afford the constant replacement that industry finds necessary. This constant falling-behind—

due to become even more pronounced in succeeding years of the new technology—invites institutionalization of obsolescence. Elimination of such instructional facilities would probably make vocational and technical programs too academic or theoretical for the tastes and aptitudes of many of the students it serves. There are no easy answers to this problem. Certainly much new thinking must be devoted to vocational and technical pedagogy, a realm visited by very few educators for a great many years. Perhaps the time is here for the educational community (with its over-all experience in matters of teaching and learning) and industry (which has many of the facilities to do the job) to re-examine their long-standing antipathy toward involvement in such questions.

Prestige. The problems in vocational and technical education are compounded by the present program's low prestige. Its students too often are the dropouts or castoffs of the academic curriculum. Its teachers, often less academically oriented, enjoy relatively low status within the teaching profession in many states. Its buildings are often the oldest, its facilities frequently the poorest, its extracurricular programs usually the weakest. Its subject matter suffers from the general debasement of manual and blue-collar occupations in contemporary social values.

These generalizations are quite unfair to the several outstanding vocational and technical programs in this country. But the generalizations persist, and almost all programs find themselves typed to the extent that their struggle is uphill. And because criticisms are applied more readily to the older vocational programs, there is an undercurrent in some quarters to disassociate the newer technical programs from their vocational counterparts, to seek a separate and more lustrous identity.

The low repute of a program is harmful in many ways: good students shy away, teachers are difficult to recruit, industry remains standoffish, other educators show little interest, and money is difficult to come by. Vocational and technical educators, faced with the dangers of indifference to or suspicion of the program, often devote more time to self-protection than to self-improvement. It is pointless to argue who is to blame. Vocational and technical education cannot solve their problems alone. A step forward would be a national recognition of the real importance of this field within the scope of the total educational effort needed for the years ahead. The Vocational Education Act of 1963 is a hopeful portent.

Teachers. The recruitment of competent teachers, difficult at all educational levels, is especially so in vocational and technical education. Teachers in this area, particularly with the program's present emphasis on shop instruction and job expertise, must themselves have a high level of job knowledge and experience. But the good skilled craftsman or technician can earn far more in industry than he can within the present salary scale of a public school teacher (a commentary in itself).

Only within vocational agriculture and home economics do the colleges graduate a good number of people each year who are qualified to teach these subjects. In other vocational and technical areas the problem is acute. The most common "solution" has been to take the willing craftsman or technician (often an older worker or other person whose earning power in industry has become limited), run him through three or six credits of education courses (for teaching techniques), and put him in front of a class.

This solution creates some difficulties: the new instructor's subject-matter knowledge tends to be circumscribed by his job experience. That experience may include little acquaintance with the related skills and knowledge that should be taught. The instructor may not have had much formal or informal education in mathematics, English, speech, industrial relations, or civic and cultural matters. Then, too, he may not be abreast of newer thinking in his field. By the same token, once he settles into the teaching routine, he tends to be isolated from newer developments in industry, for he will find few opportunities or publications to help update his knowledge.

To relate this situation is to present the need for new thinking about the preparation of vocational and technical teachers. The assumption has been that it is better to convert a journeyman into a teacher than to have a teacher acquire the necessary skills and related knowledge. Perhaps within the present situation this assumption is warranted, at least to the degree that shop-oriented instruction does require shop-oriented instructors, and to the degree that such instructors may have greater empathy with their students than the person who has never worked in a production job. However, the future role of shop- and lab-oriented instruction and the potentialities of a work-study program of teacher preparation suggest that cooperatively higher education and industry could bring about important breakthroughs in vocational and technical teaching. This is particularly true of teaching on the technical and semiprofessional level, where content and level of instruction lessen the experience and empathy factors.

No final answers are available, but the expansion and improvement of vocational and technical education are heavily dependent on some resolution of the teacher-training question. This cannot and will not happen through the efforts of people already in the field; higher education in particular must assume leadership in the preparation of vocational and technical teachers.

Guidance. The present inadequacy of guidance activities is illustrated by the fact that close to half of the states receiving Federal funds for their programs spend less than 1 percent of that money on occupational guidance and counseling. The problem begins in college-oriented high school guidance departments, which too often are staffed by people who have neither the knowledge to help students select an occupation nor the inclination to direct them toward the appropriate vocational or technical education opportunities. It continues once the student arrives in the vocational or technical school; although *no* other segment of education has recognized the importance of *vocational* guidance to the extent that these schools have, lack of funds, of reliable testing materials, and of appropriately trained *vocational* guidance counselors limits what the vocational and technical school is able to do.

As indicated earlier, the occupational life of the young person will be largely determined by the kind and level of education he receives. Student decisions are therefore crucial ones. They will, in effect, determine whether vital manpower needs will be met, whether human resources will be equal to economic potential. Further, the student's decision about his education will to a large extent define his future occupational role. But student knowledge of the world of work is today quite circumscribed, inasmuch as most work situations are unseen and unknown to young people. Only proper guidance within the educational system can direct the necessary numbers of qualified people into them.

It is also important that vocational and technical education, ever with its attention on the longer-term regional and national employment situation, help its graduates find meaningful entry into the world of work, work not necessarily near the school. Once the student is placed, it will be equally important that the bond between the school and the worker be maintained; the school must alert him to opportunities for continuing education and updating, and be prepared to re-educate and re-enter him into the work world as technology makes this necessary. Such a continuing relationship between the institution, the graduate, and his work career already exists in many of the better professional schools within higher education. It must be extended to a broader range of occupations.

2. The Development of Vocational and Technical Education

A COMPREHENSIVE HISTORY OF vocational education has yet to be written. The lack is indicative of the attitude of the academic world toward vocational education. And it also leaves too many educators in the dark about how and why this unique movement in American education came to the position in which it finds itself.

The position of this form of education is heavily rooted in the decades preceding World War I. Although the advance of democratic thought and technological innovation may have made the coming of vocational education inevitable, the actual evolution of this form of education was largely circumstantial. These circumstances are of an earlier day, and for purposes of present understanding it is now necessary to look more closely at them.[1]

VOCATIONAL EDUCATION

The concept of "vocation" is nothing new. People have always had to make certain career choices, and have tended to dignify that choice by referring to it as a "calling," or "vocation." But whether labeled as a "choice" or a "calling," until fairly recent times a person's occupation was largely determined by birth. And whether the young person became a priest, or a craftsman, or a farmer, he recognized his vocation as something permanent, or for life.

Since the life's work of the son was usually the same as his father's,

[1] The story of the development of vocational and technical education in this country is largely that of the development of vocational education. Only in the last two decades has *technical* education assumed an identity that permits it to be discussed apart from vocational education. The present status, traditions, and problems of the two are so rooted in the historical development of vocational education that the larger part of this chapter must be written as the history of *vocational* education. Some comments on the development of technical education are made at the end of this chapter.

38

the son learned the rudiments of that work from his father and from other men in the community, generally by pickup methods, involving observation, imitation, and personal initiative. In the larger commercial centers, a few skills were transmitted in a more organized manner through apprenticeship.

This state of vocational affairs was well suited to a society whose institutions—religious, political, cultural, economic, and social—were based on *permanency*. But beginning in the sixteenth century, slowly picking up momentum during the seventeenth and eighteenth, making great strides during the nineteenth, and accelerating at full tilt during the twentieth century, a countertrend developed, a trend best described by the word *change*. The idea of a single religious orthodoxy was the first of the major Western assumptions to fall. Art, music, and literature followed in breaking with traditional forms of expression. The divine right of kings lost its grip on the Western mind and new political arrangements evolved. And the industrial revolution brought new meanings to the words "industry," "trade," and "commerce." Change, and not permanency, became the mark of any institution that was to survive.

Each of these revolutions, and the industrial revolution in particular, wrought great changes between man and his work. The spread of machines and the finding of new sources of power meant that tasks formerly requiring physical strength soon required manipulative skill, and these in turn began to require knowledge of the why as well as of the how. For increasing numbers of men the pursuit of a vocation involved more than observation, imitation, and initiative; it meant, first, some particular vocational training and, eventually, some formal vocational education.

The father-son, pickup method of vocational preparation was doomed. In a factory and office system, geared to change and increasingly marked by specialization, the son was not necessarily going to do the same work his father had done. Nor, with the spread of mechanical and technological innovation, could there be any guarantee that the father knew and could pass on enough to carry the son through a life of changing work. The son needed new training, and he needed it from a new place.

Nineteenth-century Europe.   Over the nineteenth century, then, this former function of the home and neighborhood became one of the factory. As long as labor was abundant and machines were simple, training was an easy matter. The foreman was initially responsible for this function. But who was to train the foreman? And where were the workers with the middle-level skills necessary to maintain and complement the machines, people trained in the trades and crafts? These were people not readily or properly trainable "on the floor." As early as one hundred and fifty years ago many Europeans saw that this function would have to be discharged by schools, schools worthy of community support.

The nineteenth century saw rapid advances in "vocational" [2] education in Europe. Programs were begun early in the century in Prussia, in part in an effort to overcome the commercial lead of the British. These early efforts recognized the value of the social and economic efficiency in vocational training—the effect of bringing the best training to the largest number of people in the shortest possible time and, thereby, of increasing the national resources of skilled manpower. Then, as now, farsighted men realized that the country that organizes its human talents into the greatest reservoir of skills will assume an industrial and commercial advantage. Such a reservoir has always been of extreme importance to countries with limited natural resources, and the Germans were quick to sense this key to British and Dutch success. By the end of the century the German *Technikum* and the continuation school were models for vocational educators around the world.

During the mid-nineteenth century many other European nations had developed systems of vocational education. The British, then the Austrians, Swedes, Italians, French, and Russians moved into this area, often adapting the German models to their own needs. This education took the form of anything from a garage school for mechanics or craft instruction in a loft to relatively large experimental farms, industrial training centers, and university-sponsored work in the sciences. The number of students was not large, but grew steadily in proportion to the total number of students in all schools. The notable point is that these forms of vocational training became recognized as a legitimate form of *education,* one worthy of public and industrial support.[3]

---

[2] The use of the word "vocational" was not widespread in the greater part of the nineteenth century. "Useful," "practical," "utilitarian," "scientific," or "technical" were often used synonymously, all to distinguish occupationally oriented forms of education from the predominant classical curricula.

[3] The material in the preceding sections is largely adapted from Charles A. Prosser and Charles R. Allen, *Vocational Education in a Democracy* (New York: Appleton-Century, 1925).

Early America.　No such growth in vocational forms of education occurred in America prior to the Civil War. Voices were raised and a few schools launched, but it remained for the passage of the Morrill Act in 1862 to stimulate any real start.

Education in early America was dominated by British thought and practice. The nine colonial colleges, the Latin grammar schools, and the dame schools all reflected English models, with curricula centered on the Greek and Latin classics. Against this aristocracy-oriented education at least two notable voices of dissent are recorded, those of Benjamin Franklin and Thomas Jefferson.[4] Franklin had little taste for "useless classics," favoring a more utilitarian approach through which the application of science could raise the level of farming and the trades in the Colonies. Jefferson, although not condemning the value of a literary education, did take recognition of the value of "scientific" farming and training in the crafts in his 1806 proposal for a program of land-grant support of a national university.

But such suggestions received little approval in the educational community of the new Republic. The tone of education was set by the colleges, small, sectarian, patterned after European models, with curricula preserved from earlier centuries. Theology, philosophy, Latin and Greek, mathematics, and rhetoric were the courses offered, and ministers, schoolmasters, doctors, lawyers, and a few men of business were the clientele. Although strained varieties of economics, literature, history, and science were gradually added to the curriculum during succeeding decades of the nineteenth century, the subject matter was not related to practical application. Libraries were small and little used; basic and applied research were almost unknown, science was in a book and not the laboratory, and graduate study was something the wealthier went to Europe for. The public schools that did exist were cut from the same cloth, and were college preparatory in direction.

Although the Jacksonian period produced a rising chorus of voices calling for the teaching of more "practical" and "useful" knowledge in the schools, the attitude of the overwhelming majority of educators was summed up by the declaration of the Yale faculty in 1829: "There are

---

[4] Merle Curti, *Social Ideas of American Educators: Report of the American Historical Association Commission on the Social Studies,* Part 10 (New York: The Association, 1935), pp. 34–47.

many things important to be known, which are not taught in colleges, because they may be learned anywhere."

Ante-bellum America. But there were those who pointed out that the "many important things" were *not* being learned, *anywhere.* Thomas Clemson testifies that he went to Europe in 1826 because "there is not a single scientific institution on this continent where a proper scientific education can be obtained." In 1838 Solon Robinson wrote in the *Albany Cultivator:* "We should have . . . a well founded agricultural school . . . which . . . will be *useful.* Not a piano, French, Spanish, or Flower daub education, but one that will make . . . scientific farmers and mechanics, and intelligent public officers." And Francis Wayland, in the far-reaching report to the Brown University Corporation in 1850, tartly remarked, "Our colleges are not filled, because we do not furnish the education desired by the people."

Many local attempts to furnish such education are recorded. Generally, 1826 is recognized as the beginning of the American lyceum movement, a device for popular adult education through lectures; "scientific farming" was a frequently heard topic. In 1823 the first school devoted entirely to practical studies,[5] the Gardiner Lyceum in Maine, was opened. Though it lasted but ten years, scores of similar institutions were launched in succeeding years. But most of them, lacking an adequate financial basis and facing the distrust of farmer and mechanic, did not last long.

In 1824 what is now Rensselaer Polytechnic Institute opened its doors with the avowed purpose of applying "science to the common purposes of life,"[6] a truly revolutionary design in the collegiate scheme of things of that day, and of many to come. The charter of the University of Michigan (1837) provided specifically for instruction in "practical farming and agriculture," though this part of the university's

[5] As noted earlier, nineteenth-century vocational terminology can be confusing. For example, the use of the word "practical" to describe the Gardiner curriculum is to describe a curriculum consisting of classes in surveying, navigation, farming, carpentry, civil architecture, and chemistry. The history of what is now science, engineering, agricultural, vocational, and technical education in this country can be told in much the same terms up through the Civil War.

[6] Wrote Rensselaer, "My principal object is to qualify teachers for instructing the sons and daughters of farmers and mechanics . . . in the application of experimental chemistry, philosophy, and natural history to agriculture, domestic economy, the arts, and manufactures. . . ."

purpose was neglected for many years. A Farmer's Institute was founded in Cincinnati in 1846; more publicity than program seemed to result. The same was true of the People's College, opened in 1858 in Upstate New York; Horace Greeley, Mark Hopkins, and 8,000 others were in attendance at its dedication, but it did not survive the start of the Civil War. The Lawrence Scientific School at Harvard (1847) and the Sheffield School at Yale (1859) had little immediate impact on the course of their respective colleges. During the 1850's a few colleges created professorships in agricultural or scientific fields, but no substantial programs ensued. A more hopeful development was the founding of separate state-supported agricultural schools in Michigan (1855), Pennsylvania (1855), and Maryland (1859), and plans for similar schools in Iowa and Massachusetts.

By 1860 no more than 20 institutions had science curricula, and the census for that year showed that only 3 percent of the 397 American colleges had formal departments of science and agriculture.[7]

Why was this so? Two principal reasons may be assigned.

The first involves an application of the law of supply and demand. As noted earlier, Europe found that its limited natural resources demanded that greater attention be paid to its resources of human skill. America, on the other hand, was a land of great natural resources. Thus, while "scientific farming" had its advocates, a rich soil and benevolent climate seemed to ensure good crops, dulling demand for better techniques. Similarly, the country's commercial life was centered on the rich and seemingly inexhaustible resources of the forest, the mine, the field, and the sea, and as a supplier of raw materials rather than as a processer, the country could afford to neglect development of human skills and still remain prosperous. At the same time many of the needed skills in the crafts and trades were brought to these shores by increasing waves of immigrants. In short, the economic impulse toward vocational education was missing.

The second reason involves the pattern of education itself during much of the nineteenth century. Mention has already been made of curricula tied to the classics; the purpose of education, as seen by those involved in it, was to preserve and extend the general culture. But as much as this opposition from above inhibited the growth of vocational

[7] Edward D. Eddy, Jr., *Colleges for Our Land and Time* (New York: Harper & Row, 1956), pp. 6–22.

influences in the schools, it also produced an opposition from below to such a growth. The self-made man of the farm or shop had a distrust of any attempt to mix his practical ways with the prevailing pattern of education. So, despite the increasing frequency of calls for more useful and practical education, there was little popular support for such education. The great majority of the vocational institutions that were set up before the Civil War failed for lack of student and community acceptance.

The Morrill Act of 1862. This was the setting—changing, to be sure, but slowly—when President Lincoln signed the Morrill Act in 1862. The act provided grants of land to endow, support, and maintain state colleges devoted to the agricultural and mechanic arts, to "promote the liberal and practical education of the industrial classes in the several pursuits and professions of life." The provisions of the act are familiar, but it would be well to consider their relationship to what has been said.

The Morrill Act was not passed on the crest of an inexorable wave of public opinion or of pressure from powerful interest groups. On the contrary, most farmers were ignorant of its meaning and even of its passage, no significant industrial support is recorded, educators had almost no voice in its passage, and Lincoln had no recorded opinions on it. Historians agree that neither Senator Justin Morrill, who sponsored the bill, nor the influential Senator Benjamin Wade, who guided it through Congress, had any clear idea of its educational implications. Passage was sparked by a vaguely defined need to do something for the farmer,[8] who had been overlooked in the legislative largesse of earlier Congresses, and to provide a framework within which officers and engineers could be trained for the war effort; congressional debate focused on Western fears of an Eastern land grab and the question whether education was a Federal responsibility.[9]

Despite the unpromising beginnings of the Morrill Act, it had many long-range, salutary effects. It was the keystone in the development of some three score institutions of higher education, many of great learning and prestige. These institutions provided leadership, training, and research in legally assigned fields that have proved of great importance to

[8] In the middle of the last century three-fourths of the national labor force was engaged in agricultural occupations.

[9] Eddy, *Colleges for Our Land and Time,* pp. 26–44.

this nation's growth. Beyond this, though, they induced a major redirection in the pattern of American education, with at least five implications of consequence for vocational and technical education:

1. A liberal *and* practical education was prescribed. The two were not to be placed in separate camps. The classical studies were integrated into curricula that were plainly vocational, and both were to be accommodated without any sense of inferiority.

2. As the financial and philosophical basis of the state university systems, they opened the doors of higher education to a far wider public, removing forever the idea of a single education for a select few.

3. The act gave important status to the mechanic arts and agriculture, and, with the useful-practical controversy as part of its background, greatly changed the college-level teaching of these courses and of the other sciences. Science was to be taught, not just for its own sake, but as an instrument for molding the societal environment.

4. The new form of education broke through the suspicions and fears of education of farmers and businessmen. The resistance to agricultural and mechanic education in the colleges, noted earlier, gradually was overcome by the extension programs, experimental farms, and the success of graduates over the first two decades of the operation of the new colleges. This acceptance of vocationalism in the colleges was to have much significance in the later movement to extend vocationalism into the public schools.

5. The role of the agricultural colleges in improving agriculture in this country was so dramatic and so widely recognized that this new form of education came to be accepted as vital to the national welfare, as a spur to economic growth. The social efficiency of vocational education was proved to a "show me" people.

Emergence of the high school.   The years after the Civil War were ones of unprecedented growth for the reunited Republic. Immigrants came in a vast influx, and as cities filled up, so did the West. Tariffs were comfortably high, labor was plentiful and cheap, raw materials were abundant, and a spreading network of railroads was opening new markets for an expanding economy. Over the last three decades of the century the country doubled its population and tripled its gross national product. Change was coming, and new demands were to be made on the country's educational system. These demands found their first expression in the 1880's, with the initiation of a form of vocational education on the secondary level.

Why did vocationalism reach into the colleges at a relatively early date, yet take so long to be introduced into the high schools? One reason is that the colleges, from their earliest days through the latter part of the nineteenth century, enrolled a teen-age student body—students at a time of life when they were most susceptible to learning the middle-level skills demanded by society at the time. Considering the age of the students, the course content, and the level of instruction, the early land-grant colleges performed a function similar to that of a good comprehensive high school today.

Where did this leave the high school? It was not necessarily a four-year institution; many high school graduates were youngsters from the grammar schools who had been pushed through one or two years of the feeder schools that most colleges found it necessary to maintain. But, whether the high school was one year or four years, public or private, its purpose was college preparatory. It was *not* terminal in function, but simply the step in the educational ladder between the elementary school and higher education. In 1870, for example, eight out of ten high school graduates entered college, where six of them received degrees; there were more than twice as many college graduates in the country as there were people with high school diplomas only.

This state of affairs was drastically altered between 1880 and 1920. Beginning in 1880 more and more young people entered high school, and more and more stayed in high school to graduate. The 1870's saw attendance and graduation increases that barely kept pace with the over-all growth in population; after 1880 census figures show a doubling of both total enrollment and graduates for every decade that followed, up through 1930. College enrollments, on the other hand, grew much more slowly. While nearly 60 percent of the 1870 high school graduates went on to earn college degrees, the figure fell to 25 percent just after 1900, to below 20 percent during World War I, and to about 15 percent by 1940. In short, over this span of years the high school became the terminal point in the education of most American youth.

This growth and changing role of the high school had a profound effect on American higher education, especially on the land-grant colleges. As the number of high school graduates increased and as the colleges became better established, they were able to demand a four-year high school course for admission; and with a better prepared and more mature student body, they were able to upgrade their work substantially. Also, the growth of graduate study in this country during the 1880's showed the land-grant colleges how much basic work needed to be done in their indigenous agriculture- and industry-related studies, and new research and graduate work exerted an upward pull on the undergraduate curricula. Thus during the 1880's courses in farming became courses in agricultural science, and the mechanic arts grew into engineering.

The colleges had blazed the vocational trail, but as they advanced the level of their work into the highly skilled and professional areas, they left a vacuum in the field of middle-level vocational preparation. In retrospect, it was logical that this vacuum would be filled by the emerging high school. If, indeed, vocational preparation for middle-level skills is a legitimate and necessary educational function, properly discharged during the terminal phases of the student's formal education and while he is in his late teens, then the high school should have taken up this societal function that the land-grant colleges had performed over the first two or three decades of their existence. But no such ready transition was to take place. Politics, pedagogy, and the familiar pressures of tradition and status stood in the way. Over the span of the next three decades, however, the pressure to fill this middle-level-skill vacuum was built up until finally society *demanded* that it be filled, and by the schools. The traditional thinking in the high school was broken through only by means of the same extraordinary (for that time) remedy that had been used on the colleges—Federal legislation.

Resistance to vocational education. The tremendous growth in enrollments during the 1880's brought new problems of teachers, facilities, programs, and methods to the high school. The majority of the school districts in the United States still ran one-teacher schools. The teachers themselves were inadequately educated and woefully underpaid. In many large cities school administration and construction were hopelessly entangled in politics and graft. Class sizes expanded to unmanageable proportions. During the late 1880's and the 1890's, the popular magazines vied with one another in telling the public how bad its schools were. Public acceptance of education was rising, but its confidence in the schools was not.

A growing portion of criticism of the schools was coming from the pedagogical arena. Many people were beginning to realize that as the high school became for more students the terminal point of education, it would have to do more than prepare students for college. But the dominant pedagogy of the day resisted any such development. Its chief spokesman was William T. Harris, chief architect of the St. Louis school system (1868–80) and later United States Commissioner of Education (1889–1906).

Harris, well schooled in Hegel and Emerson, was convinced that the purpose of public education was to "preserve and save our civil order." The school was the "great instrumentality to lift all classes of people into a participation in civilized life," meaning order, self-discipline, civic loyalty, and a respect for private property. The school was to reflect the wisdom of the race, and teach only those things precisely defined as having a general theoretical relationship to that over-all wisdom. The classics, languages, and mathematics constituted the secondary curriculum, just as they properly formed the still-dominant basis of the college curriculum. The school prepared the student for the "work of life." [10]

The 1880's, however, were not a period in which many people could be concerned about the "work of life." Most young people of high school age were already deeply involved in a life of work. Many coal mines and textile mills and certain other factories counted more than half their workers under seventeen years of age. Massachusetts was proud of a law limiting children under twelve to a ten-hour workday. And despite the increase of school attendance in the cities, in 1890 only 7 percent of the nation's fourteen- to seventeen-year-olds were in high school.

Although the reasons for this low high school attendance record were largely social and economic, they also involved considerable indifference on the part of the students and parents toward the traditional education offered; it was something many were sure they could do as well without. The educational requisites for most of the jobs available were almost nonexistent. Students in school were reported to lack interest in much of the subject matter they were forced to memorize and repeat—subject matter dull and of little relevance to the world of work. An anti-Harris

[10] See Curti, *Social Ideas of American Educators,* chap. 9, and Lawrence A. Cremin, *The Transformation of the School* (New York: Alfred A. Knopf, 1961), pp. 14–20.

current began to run during the 1880's in educational circles. Generally it took the form of an opposition to bookish education, a reaction away from the concept of the learner as one engaged in passive absorption and toward the idea of his active appropriation of knowledge.

The manual training movement.   It was in this period of educational unrest that the manual training movement appeared in 1880. In that year, Calvin W. Woodward opened a manual training school in St. Louis. He proposed that education "put the whole boy in school, his hands as well as his head." Manual work would discipline the "mechanical faculties," while the classics did their work on the "mental." One of Woodward's colleagues, President Runkle of the Massachusetts Institute of Technology, added that "without teaching any trade we teach the essential mechanical principles of all." Manual training was *not* conceived of as vocational training. Rather it was an attempt to infuse new vitality into old curricula, to rouse student interest in school programs, to promote more sensible occupational choices, to raise the educational level of the labor classes, and to elevate all occupations to a millennium of culture and refinement.[11]

One additional aspect of the manual training movement—the development of shop instruction—deserves attention. An early problem faced by teachers of the mechanic or manual arts was how to make their training as practical as possible. In Germany, France, and England two plans were frequently used: one located the school in an industrial area so that an intimate combination of teaching and actual contact with working conditions could be established; a second required students to spend certain periods of time working in industry. For a variety of reasons neither plan was quite appropriate for the American institutions then venturing to offer practical studies. But a third European plan, from Russia, did seem appropriate. This involved the construction of shops *in the schools,* shops in which actual industrial conditions were simulated as closely as possible. The various mechanic arts were broken down into their component skills and taught in systematic order. Runkle, when he saw an exhibit of the Moscow Imperial Technical School shops at the 1876 Philadelphia Centennial Exposition, was enthusiastic, and hastened to set up a similar instructional scheme at M.I.T. Shop instruction went on to become a vital part of mechanic arts and engineering curricula of the

---

[11] *Ibid.,* pp. 28–29.

next two decades. The shop system, which at once claimed to be a democratic recognition of the importance of the industrial classes and of the learning-by-doing theories of Rousseau and Pestalozzi, was adopted by Woodward as the pedagogical heart of his manual arts program. The shop remains an important part of the legacy of the manual arts to vocational education.

The manual training movement made rapid strides during the 1880's. Privately financed schools were set up in Chicago, Cleveland, Cincinnati, New Orleans, New York, and several other cities. At the same time a few cities (Baltimore, Philadelphia, St. Paul) set up public manual training schools. Many other communities added manual training to the general school program. Cooking, carpentry, and sewing were the most frequently taught subjects. Despite the continued opposition of W. T. Harris and others, by the end of the decade manual training as envisioned by Woodward and Runkle had won its place in the schools. It survives today as the father of present-day industrial arts programs.

Vocationalism: the opening wedge.　The manual training movement also was the opening wedge for entry of vocational training into the secondary school curriculum. The line between the teaching of industrial arts and the teaching of industrial skills is a thin one, and during the 1890's a new breed of educators, less tied to the culturist tradition and pointing to the work of the land-grant colleges, was willing to cross that line. In the same sense students and their parents, more impressed with the employment opportunities held out by vocational education than by the grand design of the traditionalists for a common culture, were eager to cross the line. In the final reckoning, however, the burgeoning manpower demands of American industry resolved the issue in favor of vocationalism. During the two decades after 1890 the number of schools offering recognizably vocational programs rose from almost none into the hundreds. Many of these were proprietary schools; many were separately established public secondary schools; a few were made a part of established high school programs. Metalworking took the place of woodworking, programs in home economics were expanded, carpentry led the way to instruction in other trades, and forms of business education were widely adopted.

Such unabashed vocationalism gave rise to a new debate. Whereas even the culturists somehow could come to accept that in Woodward's manual training, with its "abstractions from all trades," there was some value for the work of life, they saw in the new vocational programs a horse of a different color. The new programs seemed to dispense with universal abstraction in favor of narrow, wholly utilitarian training. It is difficult to generalize to what extent this reaction was justified, particularly when there were so few programs, no two of which were alike; but many public educators did divide into two warring camps, the one demanding a new education for a new industrial age, the other setting up an uncompromising defense of the traditional curriculum as the only hope for the survival of general education.

The significance of this division in educational thought cannot be overestimated. During the decades 1890–1910 vocationalism was one of the hottest issues in education, and the failure of educators during that period to agree on the place of vocationalism in the schools was to leave a heavy mark on the kind of vocational education which, inevitably, was put in the schools. It was a problem to which John Dewey directed some of his most penetrating thought. Sensing the inherent danger of a developing dualism in the educational system, Dewey strongly urged the integration of vocational education into the general school program, stressing the benefits that would accrue to both forms of education, to the worker-citizen, and to the democratization of industry.[12]

But Dewey's voice was to no avail. The traditionalists refused to bend on such matters as the necessity of an academic curriculum for all students and requirements for teacher certification; many simply cringed at the sound of hammers and saws in the school. The vocationalists in turn were uncompromising in their demands for a new approach to the education of high school youth; increasingly they aligned themselves with early advocates of progressive education on such matters as curriculum diversity and classroom methodology. The gap was further widened by certain changes in the manual arts programs during the 1890's; the vocationalists complained that these had been "diluted" and "removed from reality" once they were put in the unsympathetic hands of the generalists. Many of the more pragmatic vocationalists began to advocate a *separate* public vocational high school system, one accommodating a separate kind of education in which, quite candidly, work efficiency in an industrial

---

[12] For a discussion of Dewey's views see Curti, *Social Ideas of American Educators,* pp. 499–541. The views of many earlier educators on the subject are outlined on pp. 310–498 of the same work.

democracy would be held more important than the cultural values of education.[13]

Management and labor also divided sharply over vocational education. To management, vocational training in the schools was not only a valuable source of skilled manpower, but also a way toward freeing itself from the growing union control of apprenticeship.[14] Conversely, labor, from Samuel Gompers on down to the rank and file, saw such training in the schools as an attempt by management to break unions, to use young scabs from the schools to undermine the few hard-won gains it had made.[15] Much of the history of the early vocational schools involves ticklish attempts to tread a line that would retain the support (both political and financial) of industrialists and of the unions, who controlled the needed instructors and the entry of graduates into the labor market. The founding of the National Association of Manufacturers in 1897 widened the gulf between these embattled forces.

Many of the same battles were being fought on the farm. Generally, though, the tone of debate and the actual accomplishment lagged a decade or two behind what was being done in the cities. The depressed state of American agriculture through the 1880's and most of the 1890's and the populist struggles in politics tended to distract attention from educational effort. Too, the growth of secondary education in rural America was slow, and what might have been done vocationally on that level was being done largely by the expanded extension and demonstration programs of the land-grant colleges.

Much of the rural educational effort during the 1880's was, in fact, directed to expanding these extension and demonstration programs; the passage of the Hatch Act (1887) and Second Morrill Act (1890) resulted. Also during that decade close to two dozen states set up farmers

[13] A 1908 symposium at the annual meeting of the National Education Association was the occasion for an airing of many of these issues; see N.E.A. *Journal of Proceedings and Addresses of the 46th Annual Meeting,* 1908 (Washington: The Association, 1908), pp. 155–94. Other contemporary statements of the problem include James E. Russell, "The Trend in American Education," *Educational Review,* XXXII (June 1906), 28–41, and Arthur A. Dean, *A State Policy of Promoting Industrial Education* (Albany, N.Y.: 1910), p. 68. See also Curti, *Social Ideas of American Educators,* pp. 559–60.

[14] Cremin, *The Transformation of the School,* pp. 35–36.

[15] *Ibid.,* pp. 35–38; for a contemporary statement see Edward W. Bemis, "Relation of Labor Organizations to the American Boy and to Trade Instruction," *Annals of the American Academy of Political and Social Science,* V (1894–95), 209–41.

institutes—small, shaky, publicly (but poorly) financed, of about high school level, but important forerunners of vocational education for rural America. The 1890's were a period of some growth and much debate, the land-grant colleges and farmers institutes consolidating their footholds, while the National Grange, farm journals, the Association of American Agricultural Colleges and Experiment Stations, and the American Association of Farmers' Institutes Workers, all concerned with broader development in the field, called for a farm-centered secondary education. But it was not until the first decade of this century that a rural demand for vocational education reached a climax. The teaching of agriculture in a public secondary school seems to have started in Elyria, Ohio, in 1902. Progress thereafter was slow but steady, accompanied by many speeches and editorials demanding "useful" and "practical" education on the high school level.

The strenuous age. The question of vocational training, of a useful and practical education for American youth, became less academic after 1900. By every conceivable index, the years between 1900 and 1910 were ones of great growth. The population increased from 76 million to over 92 million. The gross national product more than doubled. Farm income, after two lean decades, rose sharply. Boosts in industrial production ranged from 85 to 160 percent. Along with the accelerating social and economic changes came new demands from both the factory and the farm for skilled workers and managers. Up to 1900 a good deal of this demand had been met by the steady stream of skills provided by Northern European immigration; but the nine million immigrants who arrived in America between 1900 and 1910 were largely people from Italy, Russia, and Eastern Europe, few of whom possessed the skills demanded by the changing economy.

During the early 1900's, then, the need for skilled manpower became critical. The country turned to its school system for an answer. Educational decisions *had* to be made during these years and *were* made, not because of educational consensus but rather societal pressure to get a job done.

A coalition is formed. Management, labor, and agriculture would all stand to gain by the spread of vocational education. Yet their tripartite antipathy gradually developed as a block to such education. Labor and management could not agree on urban programs and had little interest in rural programs; and rural-dominated state legislatures were not going to vote money for vocational programs since most of the eligible schools would be in the cities.

In 1906 two forward-looking educators, Charles R. Richards of Teachers College, Columbia University, and James P. Haney, director of the New York City public school manual training program, broke the static situation by organizing the National Society for the Promotion of Industrial Education. Its purpose was plainly political—the unification of the forces tending toward vocational education throughout the country. Its first object was the reconciliation of labor-management attitudes. This was accomplished by 1910. After much prodding and debate, after many committee meetings and tours of schools, the American Federation of Labor was brought to lend its support to vocational education. In this same year the National Education Association labeled vocationalism "the central and dominant factor" in the education of youth for an industrial age. The National Grange and the Association of American Agricultural Colleges and Experiment Stations lent their resources to the movement, as did the already-committed National Association of Manufacturers. By 1910 a powerful coalition had been welded together by the National Society.

The National Society for the Promotion of Industrial Education was cut from the broad cloth of the Progressive movement. Its membership included businessmen, labor leaders, municipal reformers, settlement workers, and reformist educators. All were demanding educational experiment and reform. They were involved in what Morton White has labeled the "revolt against formalism," a formalism which to them was represented by the traditional education dominant in the schools. They protested that in the new industrial age the many functions previously handled by the family, the church, the neighborhood, or shop were *not* being performed; somehow they must get done; like it or not, the school must take them on.[16]

The gathering momentum. By 1910 the National Society could look back on more than a score of legislative conquests on the state level. In 1905 Governor Douglas of Massachusetts appointed a commission to

---

[16] Cremin, *The Transformation of the School*, p. 117. The bible of those who would make the school the center of the struggle for a better life was undoubtedly John Dewey's *School and Society* (Chicago: University of Chicago Press, 1899).

consider the appropriateness of a state-wide system of vocational education. The report of the Douglas Commission,[17] as it came to be called, is a landmark in the development of vocationalism in the public schools. Completed in 1906, the report chastised the public school system for being too exclusively literary, and said that there was a widespread interest in special training for vocations. While the commission took note of the suspicion and hostility of some labor groups, it declared that an important need for skilled workmen and greater "industrial intelligence" existed in Massachusetts industry, and that this need had to be met, and met immediately, through education at public expense. Significantly, the commission rebuked general education: "the overmastering influence of school traditions" had brought the manual arts into "subjection," so that they too had been "severed from real life as have other school activities." The general public school system could not be trusted, and so the new vocational system was *not* to be a part of the established school system. Just as the normal schools were created as separate entities to train prospective teachers, the vocational school system should afford a separate and distinct training for those electing education for specific vocational callings.

The recommendations of the Douglas Commission report were enacted into law in 1906, and a separate board was set up to administer the program. After considerable wrangling, in 1909 the program was finally placed under the general aegis of the Massachusetts State Board of Education, though duality was effectively maintained in the separate administration of the program on the local level. This duality was enhanced on the state level by the appointment in 1909 of David Snedden, a lifetime friend of vocationalism, as state commissioner of education, and of the dynamic Charles A. Prosser as state director of vocational education. Under their strong leadership the program grew rapidly and became a model for other states.

By 1910 more than a score of states followed the Bay State example and set up state-level programs of vocational education. The state legislation ran the gamut from Wisconsin's extensive plan for industrial, commercial, and agricultural training serving all parts of the state, to Illinois' permissive legislation allowing local townships to offer manual training. It was no coincidence that the state most taken up with Progressivism,

---

[17] Commonwealth of Massachusetts, *Report of the Commission on Industrial and Technical Education* (Boston: 1906).

Wisconsin, was the first to set up a truly comprehensive state-wide system of vocational education. And leaders of the movement in that state felt strongly that this form of education would develop faster and more effectively if it were administered by fully sympathetic boards and administrators. Consequently, the new system was financed and operated independently of the general school system. Although many national figures, including John Dewey, protested that a unit system was the only democratic method of organization, the very success of the Wisconsin program, once it got under way, led to its being pointed out as the "shining example" of the desirability of the "dual system." [18]

Federal aid? Up to 1910 the National Society had busied itself with promoting industrial education on the state level. Although considerable progress had been made in gaining legislative recognition on that level, progress had not been rapid enough for a program which, after all, held the key to coming to terms with a new social order. Federal aid was the answer to this pressing national need. The land-grant colleges had received their share of such aid, now why not vocational education?

In retrospect, it was an audacious plan. Almost the entire educational community was convinced that education was a state responsibility, and that in any event Federal aid would mean Federal control. But the National Society, politically activist in the Progressive tradition, was not bound by such fears. By 1912 the society's mission had become single and clear: a large-scale program of Federal assistance must be brought about. Prosser was lured from his work in Massachusetts to head the campaign. His efforts were unremitting, his success remarkable. In his first year on the job he traveled fifty thousand miles, actively advised program leaders in more than thirty states, made more than one hundred speeches in fifty cities, and became a familiar figure at the Capitol; National Society press releases and newspaper mentions could be counted in the thousands.

This campaign had its effect. By the latter part of 1913 congressional support was substantial, though probably not enough votes could have been found for passage. Vocational education bills had been introduced in every Congress since 1906, but many of the bills, including the Page-Wilson bill then before Congress, were not entirely satisfactory to the

[18] Arthur B. Mays, "50 Years of Progress in Vocational and Practical Arts Education," *American Vocational Journal,* XXXI (December 1956), 37–38.

National Society. It was also becoming clear in 1913 that influential rural interests in Congress were working at cross purposes, favoring vocational education, to be sure, but even more intent on enacting the broad agricultural extension act proposed by the Smith-Lever bill. Congressional figures and the National Society worked out a new strategy to meet this situation: the National Society would hold back on its campaign so that rural interests could concentrate their efforts on passage of the Smith-Lever bill, and in return Congress would create a national commission to study the unsolved problems of the Page-Wilson bill. Rural interests promised that once the Smith-Lever bill was adopted, they would put their full efforts behind passage of a broad vocational education bill.

This is the way it worked. In January 1914 the Smith-Lever Act was passed, the Page-Wilson bill was defeated, and the Congress authorized and the President signed a bill creating a Commission on National Aid to Vocational Education.

Commission on National Aid to Vocational Education. From the time President Wilson announced his nine appointees, the outcome was assured. Four were prominent congressional advocates of vocational education; the other five were members of the National Society for the Promotion of Industrial Education, including Dr. Prosser. Dr. Prosser himself was the guiding figure of the National Commission, and his zeal and forcefulness are evident throughout the paragraphs of its report.[19] As a statement of contemporary thought on vocational education and because of its heavy influence on subsequent legislation, this document deserves close attention. It is the Magna Carta of vocational education in the United States.

The Commission report began by outlining the need for a national program of support for vocational education. Less than 1 percent of the nation's 12,600,000 farmers had "adequate preparation for farming," while "not one in a hundred" of the 14,260,000 people in mechanical pursuits and allied industries had "any adequate chance to secure training." This was contrasted with the thirty-year-old German program; in Bavaria alone there were more trade schools than in the entire United States. This being so, the Commission went on to describe the "economic need" for vocational education. By inadequate provision for vocational

[19] U.S. House of Representatives, *Report of the Commission on National Aid to Vocational Education,* 63rd Cong., 2d Sess., H.R. Doc. 1004.

education the country was despoiling the soil, wasting labor in pools of underemployed and unemployed, hindering the growth of wage-earning power, restricting the quality and quantity of product output, raising prices with wasteful production techniques, holding down economic growth, and jeopardizing the nation's position in the world trade market. These arguments, couched in bread-and-butter terms, were designed to attract the attention of the industrialist and union man, farmer and consumer, the conservationist, and the nationalist.

The Commission also felt there was a need to "democratize" education, to recognize "different tastes and abilities," to connect culture with utility through "learning by doing" and education with life through "purposeful and useful" training in the schools. It was a progressive education catalogue of values, a panacea for crime, and a prescription to a higher standard of living for all. And for congressmen, the results of an extensive poll were presented, which showed overwhelming public sentiment for vocational education, "from the educator, the manufacturer, the trade unionist, the businessman, the social worker, and the philanthropist."

Specifically, the Commission recommended Federal-state assistance to a cooperative program of vocational education on the secondary school level, or, as the Commission put it, "of less than college grade." Teacher salary and training costs were to be federally supported, but the cost of facilities and maintenance was to be borne by the states. A minimum of 50 percent of the school time was to be given to shop work on a useful or productive basis. Agricultural, industrial, trade, and home economics offerings were to be supported. However, no particular evaluation of these offerings was made; although continually repeating that vocational training is an appropriate form of education, it did not consider what would be the most appropriate form of vocational education. The Commission's recommendations were a confirmation of the programs then in existence. Of equal significance was the recommendation that an independent Federal board be set up to administer the program in cooperation with boards to be created or designated by the states. The Office of Education was bypassed; duality was to begin at the top. Neatly mindful of good congressional and public relations, the Commission submitted its report promptly and returned $5,000 of its $15,000 congressional appropriation.

The Smith-Hughes Act. The report of the National Commission received a good press, and plans were laid to push passage of the recommended legislation when Congress convened in 1915. For reasons not altogether clear, the bill lay in congressional pigeonholes for a couple of years, despite the variety and extent of favorable testimony and committee reports. The Chamber of Commerce ringingly endorsed the measure in 1916. The Association of American Agricultural Colleges and Experiment Stations, as promised, drummed up rural support for the measure. Labor, management, social work, political, child labor, and military conventions passed strong resolutions in behalf of the bill. Leaders of the National Society combed cloakrooms for votes, and President Wilson sent three messages to Congress in behalf of the bill. In the final analysis, though, events in Europe provided the momentum to pass the bill. Late in 1916 and early in 1917 talk became more frequent about the need to "catch up with the Germans" in the training of workers for a war effort, and the vocational education bill became a "national preparedness" factor. In this setting the bill was passed in February 1917, with only one dissenting vote. It was signed by the President just two months before United States entry into the war.

The passage of the act—the Vocational Education Act of 1917, known as the Smith-Hughes Act—was received with great joy by the National Society, and the momentum of its efforts brought the provisions of the act swiftly into reality. The act created a Federal Board for Vocational Education, composed of the Secretaries of Agriculture, Labor, and Commerce, the United States Commissioner of Education, and three citizens representing industry, agriculture, and labor; it met several times during the summer of 1917. A staff was put together, largely comprised of people active in the National Society and including Dr. Prosser. By the end of the year all forty-eight states had, as the act required, submitted plans for approval; since few states had any relevant experience, these generally followed a uniform topical outline prepared by Dr. Prosser and the Federal Board staff. Because of this circumstance and the fact that the Smith-Hughes Act offered categorical aid only within narrowly defined limits, the Federal influence in the development of state programs was strong. Although the former members of the National Society now running the Federal Board could well justify this Federal dominance (which they had sought) as a means of preserving the integrity of the program from interference from hostile general educators in the states, for better or worse this Federal vocational education legislation is a prime example of the meaning and effect of "Federal control" brought about by a plan of categorical aid.

The initial Smith-Hughes authorization was $7 million. The net effect of the new program was most gratifying to friends of vocational education. Within three years enrollment in federally subsidized programs doubled, and total program expenditures, including state and local funds, quadrupled. Continued congressional support seemed to assure continuing appropriations, and the passage of compulsory school attendance laws in each of the forty-eight states by 1923 brought larger and larger numbers of students into the program. It was an age of exciting growth and experimentation, and the future promised nothing but better things to come.

The last four decades. The $7 million yearly appropriation of funds for the Smith-Hughes Act continues to this day. Prior to the passage of the Vocation Education Act of 1963 various other enactments had added some $40 million to that basic yearly sum.

The George-Reed Act (1929) was the first of these, adding $1 million annually to expand the agriculture and home economics programs. When it lapsed in 1934, the George-Ellzey Act was passed, upping the supplementary funds to $3 million, with additional support for trades and industry training. This 1934 act was succeeded in 1936 by the George-Dean Act, which added $14 million to the basic $7 million Smith-Hughes appropriation; the funds were authorized on a continuing basis, and, for the first time, distributive occupations received support. The increases came, remarkably enough, during a period of great pressure for governmental economy, when, for example, the U.S. Office of Education itself had its meager funds cut by 33 percent. Credit for this legislative success goes in large measure to the work of the American Vocational Association,[20] which has maintained the vocational education tradition of political activism that was characteristic of the original National Society. One minor setback in prestige was suffered during the 1930's, however, when

[20] In 1918, the National Society for the Promotion of Industrial Education changed its name to National Society for Vocational Education. In 1926, the new National Society merged with the Vocational Education Association of the Middle West to become the American Vocational Association, now the leading professional organization in this field.

the functions of the independent Federal Board for Vocational Education were transferred to the Office of Education.

During World War II, Congress put more than $100 million into a program called Vocational Education for National Defense (VEND), which, between 1940 and 1945, gave seven million war production workers pre-employment and supplementary training. The program received much justified praise, and vocational education received its reward in 1946 when Congress supplanted the $14 million George-Dean Act with the $29 million George-Barden Act. This act authorized funds for the same four service fields—agriculture ($10 million), home economics ($8 million), trades and industry ($8 million), and distributive occupations ($2.5 million); greater flexibility was allowed to the states in their programs. Considerable sums of money also reached vocational education programs through the GI bill.

The early 1950's were years of beleaguerment for vocational education. As the veterans finished their education, many shaky programs foundered. At this time, too, the over-all success of this country's international effort and a rising economy of full employment were taken to vindicate the work of our educational system and, in particular, reinforced the position of those favoring its general or liberal arts orientation. The argument of being "fly-by-night" was hurled at vocational programs with—actually—little justification but considerable effect. The Federal school aid controversy was at its height, and the vocational program, a conspicuous instance of Federal aid to secondary education, was caught up in the argument. Heavy spending on the Korean War brought forth demands for cutbacks in domestic spending, and states-righters said the Federal Government should get out of the program altogether. Labor and business support was lukewarm. Against these forces the A.V.A. rallied its legislative allies, and the program scraped through its yearly congressional battles with only minor damage, most of which was repaired between 1955 and 1957. In 1956 practical nursing and fishery trades were added to the George-Barden Act.

The 1958 National Defense Education Act brought the first significant addition to the program since its inception some forty years earlier. Under title VIII of the National Defense Education Act Federal funds were made available ". . . for the training of individuals designed to fit them for useful employment as highly skilled technicians in recognized occupations requiring scientific knowledge . . . in fields necessary for the national defense." The new title contemplated the support of "area vocational education programs," programs conducted by high school and post-high-school institutions of "less than college grade" serving more than one school district. Because of these restrictions the program had considerable trouble getting under way, but now seems to be functioning with a minimum of controversy. "Technical education" is a growing part of the Federal program, though thus far actual Federal appropriations ($11 million in fiscal year 1962) have been relatively small. The total 1963 Federal appropriation for vocational and technical education was just over $57 million.

Rising concern over the persistence of unemployment and underemployment in economically depressed areas has led to the recent enactment of two additional pieces of vocational legislation. Section 16 of the 1961 Area Redevelopment Act provides about $4.5 million a year for vocational training for persons in those areas the act is designed to help. The Manpower Development and Training Act of 1962 provides training programs for the unemployed and those whose skills need upgrading in order to meet shifting employment needs. In both programs the Federal Government pays 100 percent of the costs; both rely heavily on the facilities of already established vocational programs. The MDTA has enrolled some 60,000 trainees in its first year of operation, and promises to be a significant addition to the established program.

In many respects 1963 was the most exciting and important in the history of vocational education. After a year-long study by a special Presidential Panel of Consultants (the first such study since 1914), the Congress enacted the Vocational Education Act of 1963. That act is described in some detail in chapter 5 of this report. Suffice it to say that it is a major departure in vocational education legislation, containing major amendments to the Smith-Hughes and George-Barden Acts and authority for a completely new program unfettered by the restrictions of the older legislation. In time it promises a new philosophy in the relationship between education and work in the United States.

In implementing the Vocational Education Act of 1963, education will be faced with the realities of the existing structure of vocational education. That structure is the legacy of a federally supported program that for forty-six years was kept in the high-button shoes it was put in before World War I.

The legacy of history. There are many possible ways in which a nation can educate its youth, and just as many ways in which it can provide itself with skilled manpower. This country adopted a unique system of education, wherein these two societal functions were joined. Vocational preparation was defined largely in terms of the craft and the farm, and was to be a semiautonomous part of public secondary education. This particular marriage between the school and the world of work has left much to be desired, as later chapters of this report will point out.

Nothing about this marriage was preordained. In the decades and centuries before the passage of the Smith-Hughes Act many alternatives were presented to this country as it groped for answers to its problems of education and work. The choices made were more often the product of immediate circumstance than of thoughtful reflection.

The onrush of industrial and technological revolution in this country had, by the turn of the century, resolved the need for formal vocational training. Given this need, there could have been many alternative ways of meeting it. The father-son, pickup method could have been preserved, but democratic notions that tell every mechanic's son he can be President and economic demands for efficient training doomed this method to obsolescence. Apprenticeship could have been expanded, but its period of indenture runs counter to the grain of independence in too many youth, and when it became embroiled in the labor-management disputes of fifty to seventy-five years ago, it lost much of its vitality. Industry could have done the job, but the need for vocational training arose in this country at a time when industry won few stars for enlightenment, and if it could shove this function off on someone else, it was glad to do so; also the public at large had reservations about entrusting the training of its youth to the captains of industry. Organized labor could have assumed this function, but an organization fighting for its life had little time to worry about such matters. Religious, civic, and philanthropic institutions might have taken the responsibility, but it is doubtful whether in this country they have ever had the organization or money to do the job that needed to be done.

For various reasons, then, many institutions theoretically capable of providing this nation's youth with vocational training failed to do so. And so the public turned to its educational system.

There were many alternative responses the educational community could have made. In the largest sense, the alternatives involved acceptance or rejection of vocationalism in the schools, the question of whether or not to recognize vocational training as an expanding, necessary, and legitimate form of education and therefore deserving of full status and support. Put in these terms, the response of the educational community was largely negative. But the nation, facing mounting demands from a changing world of work, refused to take no for an answer. If the marriage had to be by shotgun, that was the way it had to be. Vocational education was pushed into the educational system; when it came in, it did so on its own terms.

The essentials of our present structure of vocational education are embodied in the Smith-Hughes Act. It seems odd that a study of a field closely related to a constantly and dramatically changing world of work must pay so much attention to a Federal enactment more than forty-six years old. A study of the land-grant institutions of today, for example, would make only nostalgic reference to the Morrill Act of 1862. Yet it was the Smith-Hughes Act that both quickened and prescribed the development of vocational education in the United States; that act, though supplemented by others, remained basically unchanged to 1963, as did the philosophy which nurtured it.

What was the philosophy embodied in the Smith-Hughes Act? In the largest sense, it represented a national endorsement of the appropriateness of vocational training in the schools, a recognition of the value of this form of education to the nation and the individual. In another and more important sense, however, the act's provisions embodied a vocational philosophy heavily rooted in circumstances of the decades preceding World War I.

Highlights of that vocational philosophy lie in the following concepts:

1. *Uniformity.* At the time the legislation was enacted, few school administrators had any familiarity with what the experienced vocationalists in the National Society for the Promotion of Industrial Education considered the elements of a good vocational program, and so the vocationalists made sure that those elements were written into the law. The act prescribed what courses were to be supported, and set the conditions under which they must be taught. Thus vocational education tended to become uniform in character throughout the country. More important, vocational education has tended to remain uniform down through the years, as the very detail of the act prevented Federal support for a great deal of possible experimentation with new programs.

2. *Duality*. The historic antipathy of many general educators led the early vocationalists to believe that the integrity and success of a Federal program would depend on its administration by people familiar with and sympathetic to vocational education, and consequently the act's administrative provisions were so drawn as to encourage the separate administration of the program—the duality in the educational system which Dewey and others had so strongly opposed.

3. *High school*. The drafters of the act wanted to bring vocational opportunities to the widest possible student audience. In 1917 the means lay in putting vocational education in the high school, which for the "industrial classes" served as the capstone of the educational system. The "less than college grade" provision, despite subsequent Office of Education definitions which allowed Federal money to go to post-high-school institutions, tended to keep vocational education identified as a high school function, one outside the interest or concern of higher education.

4. *Practical*. Out of the old useful-practical concept came provisions in the act that, for example, vocational agriculture students had to participate in at least six months of directed or supervised farming practice, and trades and industry students must spend at least one-half of the instruction time in shop work on a useful or productive basis. The authors of the act, bearing in mind what had happened to the manual arts, took no chance that the utilitarian aspects of the new program were going to be unduly encroached upon by hostile general educators.

5. *Terminal*. The program, with its heavy emphasis on shop-farm experience, was designed to fit its graduates for useful employment, and not for additional study beyond the high school. Any vocational program designed for credit toward the baccalaureate degree was declared ineligible for support. The program was to be terminal because it was tailored to fit into an institution, the high school, which in 1917 was the terminal point in the education of almost all students the program was designed to serve.

6. *Track*. Despite American abhorrence of European track systems, the practical and terminal provisions of the law meant that the student electing the vocational program after the ninth grade was severely limiting chances for continuing his education beyond the high school. But again, in 1917 this could hardly have been considered a problem.

7. *Farm-craft*. The vocational subjects chosen for Federal support were drawn from the particular demands of the contemporary rural and

industrial economy. Over 60 percent of the funds were channeled into vocational agriculture (apportioned among the states on the basis of farm population) and home economics (apportioned on the basis of rural population); this was in part a reflection of the need to boost secondary school education opportunities in rural America, in part a reflection of the power of rural interests in Congress at that time. The choice of homemaking as the appropriate "vocational" preparation for girls was natural in an era when a woman's place was still considered to be in the home. The emphasis on trades and crafts in industrial education was a natural response to the demands of a growing industrial economy centered on the blue-collar production worker.

8. *Shop*. The drafters of the act made the assumption that the student should be taught in a fully equipped school shop by a professional teacher with practical experience. In a period of comparatively slow technological change it was valid to assume that the institutionalization of school equipment and teacher experience would present few problems of obsolescence.

9. *Vocation*. The act, with its emphasis on relatively narrow, practical, terminal training, implicitly assumed that student preparation for future retraining is not important, that the training it gives is "vocational," or for life.

Conclusion. This, then, is where vocational education finds itself today. Obviously, many of the assumptions underlying the existing structure of vocational education need re-examination in the light of the new relationship between man, his work, and his education. The Vocational Education Act of 1963 has swept away most of the statutory underpinnings that perpetuated these assumptions, and furnishes a propitious opportunity for such a re-examination. That re-examination is the responsibility of the entire educational community. For, as this chapter has shown, both general and vocational educators bear an equal responsibility for the particular evolution of vocational education in the United States. Both bear the heavy responsibility of providing today's youth with the best education for a changing world of work.

TECHNICAL EDUCATION

A recent and significant addition to the American vocational effort has been the growth of technical education. In the last two decades technical education has assumed a separate identity that permits discussion apart from vocational education. In this sense its development is contemporary rather than historical.

The traditional home of technical education was the technical institute, generally a post-high-school, but subcollegiate, institution. The subject matter was oriented toward engineering, which it is not, and was often taught alongside vocational courses in the trades and crafts, from which it also differs. Set in this no-man's land between the high school and college, between the skilled trades and engineering, technical education has had one of the most tortured developments of any form of American education.

Early beginnings.   A few writers have attempted to trace the history of technical education back to the Gardiner Lyceum, or the old mechanics institutes, or the original curricula of the early engineering schools. Such attempts are fruitless. These nineteenth-century schools, in both conception and practice, had curricula that bore little or no relation to what we now label the "technical" occupations; all have either long since closed or turned to work in other fields.

The first recognizably technical curriculum was offered in 1895 by the Pratt Institute in Brooklyn, and was modeled closely on the German *Technikum*. This was a distinctly post-high-school institution, enrolling a mature student body with considerable industrial experience in a curriculum spread over two years. Extensive shop and laboratory work was used to integrate an intensive series of courses in mathematics, science, and the related technological subject matter. In level of instruction and nature of the student body it differed from vocational education, while in course content and manner of instruction it differed from engineering education.

For this country it was a new form of education, one that was forced to begin outside the mainstream of education, one that was not a part of the traditional educational ladder. This early technical institute and the schools that followed it were but one reflection of the contemporary growth of vocational education. Both vocational and technical education were products of essentially the same societal forces: they were designed to meet new educational needs of the industrial classes and had a common philosophy of education; they were comrades in arms in the heady push for the acceptance of vocational forms of education. Partly because of this common origin and partly because of a massive ignorance of this field, educational and popular literature had lumped them together under the heading "vocational education" until very recent times.

The development of technical education after the founding of the Pratt Institute is in no sense continuous. Its development has been marked by two major problems: the difficulty in gaining recognition that the technical represents a vital occupational area worthy of educational attention, and the difficulty in finding appropriate instructional frameworks within which to offer technical education.

The technical occupations. The major block to technical education during the last century and first three decades of this century was the failure in this country to recognize the existence of a level of work between the skilled trades and the professions, particularly engineering. Recognition has existed in Europe, and especially in Germany, for more than a century. The first glimmer did not appear in this country until around the turn of the century. The Pratt Institute was the first educational reflection of that glimmer; but twenty-five years after its founding there were still no more than a dozen technical institutes in this country.

The technician's battle for occupational recognition has now, of course, largely been won. A first turning point came in the late 1920's when the Society for the Promotion of Engineering Education undertook a thorough evaluation of engineering education in the United States. One of the most important outcomes of that historic study was the identification of technical education as an essential part of the development of the profession. The society pointed out that educational development in this field had been "most one-sided," that whereas engineering schools had been set up across the country, technical institutes were comparatively nonexistent, "their graduates had no credentials of wide acceptance, and no professional or educational bodies of wide influence extended recognition or encouragement." [21]

This was an important step forward, but only during World War II did developments enable technical education to attain appropriate recognition. The acute shortage of engineers in wartime industries led to the

[21] William E. Wickenden, *A Comparative Study of Engineering Education in the United States and in Europe* (Society for the Promotion of Engineering, 1929), pp. 251–52.

increased use of technical personnel in many areas previously considered the preserve of the professional, and the technician came to be recognized as a vital component in the engineering team. Early in the war Congress passed legislation setting up an Engineering and Management War Training Program, which, after considerable debate, made technical training a function of the higher education—and not the vocational education—branch of the U.S. Office of Education. After the war the Office of Education published *Vocational Education of College Grade,* which sharpened the distinction between technical education and vocational education (the latter, of course, being defined by law as "of less than college grade"). About the same time the Engineers' Council for Professional Development began speaking of "the engineering team," linking the technician to the near-professional level and apart from the skilled level. These and other events that followed, including industry-wide recognition that differences exist between the skilled, technical, and professional work levels, have virtually completed the process of bringing recognition to the engineering technician.

Although the technical-level occupations first received attention in the field of engineering, they have, especially since World War II, come to be recognized in an increasing number of other fields. In the medical and health services, for example, the registered nurse has taken on many of the functions previously performed by the doctor, and she in turn has relinquished many of her tasks to the licensed practical nurse. In many of the sciences, laboratory and equipment technicians are commonplace. Persons designated as "technical" now serve in such fields as construction, agriculture, personnel, merchandising, and government.

Some of the technical-level occupations prefer to call themselves "semi-professional." However, the term "technical" has been winning greater acceptance to describe this broad middle level of occupations, because many of these emerging occupations do not serve a profession as such—data processing, the office services, the applied and graphic arts, fire science, law enforcement, safety inspection, cosmetology, specialty sales, food service, and others are examples. All are of technical level in having relatively common educational requisites (one to three years of college-level study) and in requiring educational preparation that is typically more rigorous and theoretical than that for the vocational subjects, more specialized and applied than for the professional subjects.

Full recognition of the importance of the broad sweep of technical occupations within the economy has yet to be achieved. Some people still resist the application of the term "technician" to anybody but the engineering technician; others still think of the technician within the traditional vocational framework. Yet the corner has been turned in the technical occupations' struggle for recognition in the occupational spectrum.

Growth of technical education.   This heightened sense of recognition has led to a spurt in technical education efforts since World War II. But, measured in terms of assignment of appropriate institutional responsibilities, the response of education has been hopelessly scattered and unfocused.

Consider the difficulties of the engineering technologies. An illustrative starting point is the 1929 study of the Society for the Promotion of Engineering Education. It recounts that many institutions of the (engineering) technical institute type were launched in the pattern of the Pratt Institute. Yet in 1929 it could identify only eighteen reasonably sound institutions that had technical education curricula; most of these were concentrated in a few locations in the East and Midwest. Of these, four were proprietary schools, seven state-supported, and seven endowed. It found a striking lack of unity in their organization, curricula, and methods. In many of the schools technical education was a minor and ill-defined part of the over-all institutional purpose.

Why was this so? In part it was due to lack of recognition of the technical occupations and to a failure to agree on the proper form of education for them. Equally important was the institutional inconsistency of the separate technical institute, to which technical education was then tied. Evidence indicates that standards in these institutes have traditionally been high and that they have provided much of the initiative and leadership in the field. Its basic problem was that the level of work it offered was neither secondary nor baccalaureate, and it arrived on the educational scene at a time when education did not recognize that there was an intermediate terminal level. The technical institute was born and remained an educational outsider, an institution apart from the traditional ladder.

The trouble is that, for better or worse, American educational thought strongly resists the development of separate schools, and offers important status and support only to the more comprehensive institution within the educational mainstream. By this token, vocational education has suffered important losses to the degree that it has tried or been forced to construct its own dualisms. And, demonstrably, no form of American education has successfully risen in importance outside the main structure of education; Armed Forces schools, business schools, and correspondence schools have, among others, learned that apartness connotes "second class" in the public mind. The technical institute was a separate institution, and historically it was unable to carry the day for technical education.

The fate of the technical institutes founded in the first three decades of this century serves as an example of the effect of two major trends already noted: (1) the general acceptance of technical education as an appropriately educational function of the thirteenth and fourteenth grades (partly this has come about as technical education assumed its own identity and left behind the high school label of vocational education), and (2) the pressures tending toward the assimilation of technical education into the mainstream of education. The only way an engineering technical institute could integrate itself into the mainstream was by becoming a high school or by becoming a college; there appeared to be no in-between course. The choice was an obvious one, and the allurement of offering the baccalaureate degree led many of these schools to become four-year engineering colleges. Other technical institutes simply went out of business. A few were absorbed by universities. And only a handful of technical institutes remained to be founded.

In this prewar setting, viewed in retrospect, it is strange that such institutional convulsions should have occurred at all. For if technical education should be taught in the thirteenth and fourteenth grades and made a part of a comprehensive school within the educational ladder, then it should have joined hands with the two-year college, whose growth runs strikingly parallel to that of technical education. That was not to be. The junior college, in its early development, took the road of least resistance and greatest status by assuming a college-transfer function and simply duplicating the first two years of the college curriculum. This over-all picture has changed, particularly in the last ten years; nevertheless, the growth of technical education has been a recent development because of educational attitudes (reflected in the junior college) working against the establishment of terminal or occupational curricula beyond the high school and below the baccalaureate level.

The transition of the nonengineering-related technologies into the educational mainstream has encountered many of the same difficulties. Partly because of this, the response to the inevitable educational demands of the technical occupations has been inconsistent and diffuse. Technical education can now be found in some high school programs, in a growing number of postsecondary area vocational-technical schools, in special on-campus offerings of a few universities, in extension centers of several state universities, in the few dozen remaining technical institutes, in several hundred thriving proprietary schools, and in an increasing percentage of the country's community and junior colleges. All of this effort amounts to substantial recognition of the importance of an educational response to the needs of the technical occupations. But technical education still has a long way to go before it achieves the institutional recognition it deserves within education.

Conclusion. Technical education finds itself today in a position similar to that of vocational education some fifty years ago. As already pointed out, the question of need for a concerted educational effort to meet the manpower needs of the technical occupations has now been resolved. The need can be met only within the educational system, and society will insist that the job be done there. Decisions are going to be made. But whether these decisions will be made by educators acting within a consensus that this is a legitimate and necessary form of education for our time or by legislators reacting to societal pressures to get a job done is still an open question. The history of vocational education should suggest to all educators, particularly those in higher education, the importance of a vigorous, imaginative approach to the educational needs of the technical occupations.

3. Vocational and Technical Education in Secondary and Higher Education

Today's accelerating and changing technology has placed man, his education, and his work in a new relationship in which education becomes the bridge between man and his work. The difficulty, however, is that relations between education and the world of work have never been close in this country and in many respects remain in a state of bad repair.

Some understanding of the situation is provided by a review of current efforts in the United States to provide occupational education. The present chapter deals with such efforts in institutions of secondary and higher education; chapter 4, dealing with other opportunities for learning, will round out the picture. Since comprehensive data are available only for programs eligible for Federal assistance, much of the discussion in the present chapter deals with the Federal program.

The information presented in this and following chapters is, of course, based on the operation of the Smith-Hughes and George-Barden Acts, and does not reflect the potential impact of the Vocational Education Act of 1963.

SECONDARY SCHOOL LEVEL

Although the total amount of occupational education conducted in high schools is not known exactly, generally the programs are vocational in character and are offered under the aegis of the Federal vocational education program. The Federal program's enrollment figures, shown in Table 6, give a reasonable picture of vocational education enrollments in the nation's high schools.

The figures in Table 6 taken by themselves can be misleading. They include adults in part-time and evening classes and enrollees in distinctly post-high-school programs and institutions; they also fail to reflect the

73

number of graduates who complete the programs. However, examination of the individual programs within the high school vocational education

TABLE 6

Enrollment in Federally Supported Vocational and Technical Classes, by Type of Program, 1956–62

(in thousands)

Year	Total	Agri-culture	Distributive Occupations	Home Economics	Trades and Industry*	Practical Nursing	Technical Education
1962....	4,073	823	321	1,726	1,005	49	149
1961....	3,856	805	306	1,610	964	47	123
1960....	3,768	796	304	1,588	938	40	101
1959....	3,701	757	311	1,586	968	31	48
1958....	3,629	776	283	1,560	984	27	...
1957....	3,522	775	280	1,508	952	7	...
1956....	3,413	786	257	1,487	884	..	...

* Includes enrollment in fishing occupations.
Source: U.S. Office of Education, *Digest of Annual Reports of State Boards of Vocational Education, Fiscal Year Ended June 30, 1962* (Washington: Government Printing Office, 1963), p. 22. The 1962 enrollments are provisional figures, subject to final review of state reports. Figures may not add to totals because of rounding.

effort and analysis of the figures in Table 6 will assist an evaluation of the relative place of these programs in the over-all program of the high school.

Vocational agriculture. Vocational agriculture programs are carried on in some 9,600 high schools and a few junior colleges in this country. Recent enrollment figures in the Federal program are given in Table 7. The curriculum includes five major subjects: production of livestock and farm crops, marketing of farm products, farm business management, soil management, and improved citizenship and rural leadership. Instruction is carried on in the classroom, the laboratory, and through supervised farm projects for each student. Students may enroll in the ninth grade and complete the program by the end of the twelfth grade.

During the past decade agriculture enrollments have grown 8 percent, a growth that is paradoxical in face of the loss of 3 million agricultural jobs between 1947 and 1962. During this same period farm production rose 30 percent, in part because of the success of vocational agriculture programs in increasing the efficiency of the American farmer.

Vocational agriculture has, since the passage of the Smith-Hughes Act, been devoted to training "present and prospective farmers for proficiency in farming." The difficulty now is that farming opportunities are non-existent for many rural youths to the extent that only a third of the

TABLE 7

Enrollment in Vocational Agriculture Classes,
by Type of Class, 1956–62

(in thousands)

Year	All Classes	Day Classes	Evening Classes	Part-time Classes
1962............	823	474	270	79
1961............	805	463	269	73
1960............	796	464	267	66
1959............	757	466	235	56
1958............	776	462	265	49
1957............	775	458	270	46
1956............	786	460	278	47

Source: *Digest of Annual Reports of State Boards of Vocational Education, . . . 1962,* pp. 23, 34. The 1962 enrollments are provisional figures, subject to final review of state reports. Figures may not add to totals because of rounding.

70,000 yearly graduates of the vocational agriculture program remain in farming. With farm jobs vanishing at the rate of 250,000 a year, it is estimated that only one out of every ten youths now living on farms can look forward to employment on commercially profitable farms in 1970. Yet in the great majority of high schools in rural America, vocational agriculture is the only pre-employment course offered. The Vocational Education Act of 1963 will broaden the definition of vocational agriculture to include training for related agricultural occupations, such as food processing, irrigation, marketing, and farm equipment repair. At best, however, this is but a partial answer to the problem of bringing realistic pre-employment opportunities to the youth of rural America.

The 1962 Federal expenditure for vocational agriculture was about $14 million; state and local funds added another $60 million to the total program expenditure. As is the case in the Federal program's other categories, most of this money is used for the payment of salaries and the training costs of the program's instructors and supervisors.

Homemaking education. The largest federally supported vocational program in the high school is in homemaking, or home economics. In 1962 the program enrolled 1,726,000 students (see Table 8).

Homemaking curricula include courses in foods and nutrition, clothing and textiles, housing, home equipment and furnishings, child development, family relations, consumer education, and home management. The objective of the program is to prepare young people (almost exclusively girls) for the responsibilities of the home and family. Programs are available to senior high school students, youth who have left school, and adults.

Some 54 percent of the full-time enrollees in high school vocational programs are in homemaking. Some 38 percent of the total homemaking enrollment consists of part-time and evening students. Although homemaking enrollments have risen steadily over the years, relatively they have not kept pace with the over-all rise in high school enrollments.

TABLE 8

Enrollment in Home Economics Classes, by Type of Class, 1956–62

(in thousands)

Year	All Classes	Day Classes	Evening Classes	Part-time Classes
1962............	1,726	1,063	611	52
1961............	1,610	981	566	63
1960............	1,588	947	586	55
1959............	1,586	928	582	76
1958............	1,560	915	577	67
1957............	1,508	890	553	65
1956............	1,487	851	566	71

Source: *Digest of Annual Reports of State Boards of Vocational Education*, . . . *1962*, pp. 23, 40. The 1962 enrollments are provisional figures, subject to final review of state reports. Figures may not add to totals because of rounding.

Until recently homemaking education did not prepare students for payroll jobs and was, therefore, vocational only in the broadest sense of the word. The Vocational Education Act of 1963 would direct at least part of the program to pre-employment opportunities in home-related services, such as child care, food service, and interior decoration.

About half of the high schools in the nation offer federally assisted vocational home economics programs. The popularity of the program at the community level is illustrated by the fact that state and local governments have overmatched the annual $9 million Federal contribution by eight to one.

Distributive education. Distributive education includes a wide variety of programs such as retail and wholesale marketing, warehousing, trade and finance, and export-import trade. The programs are generally conducted through the high schools; some 1,300 high schools offered distributive education courses in 1961.

Until now students must already have been employed in a distributive occupation before they could enroll in a federally financed course. The Vocational Education Act of 1963 will make pre-employment programs possible. About 85 percent of the present participants are adult employees, supervisors, and managers enrolled in extension classes; the remaining enrollment comprises high school and junior college students in part-time cooperative programs (see Table 9). Total program enroll-

TABLE 9

*Enrollment in Distributive Occupations Classes,
by Type of Class, 1956–62*

(in thousands)

Year	All Classes	Extension Classes	Part-time Cooperative Classes
1962.............	321	277	44
1961.............	306	263	43
1960.............	304	264	40
1959.............	311	274	36
1958.............	283	202	80
1957.............	280	204	76
1956.............	257	173	84

Source: *Digest of Annual Reports of State Boards of Vocational Education, . . . 1962,* pp. 23, 37. The 1962 enrollments are provisional figures, subject to final review of state reports. Figures may not add to totals because of rounding.

ment is about equally divided between men and women; nearly half of the enrollment is concentrated in a half-dozen states.

Employment opportunities in the distributive occupations for well-trained personnel have expanded greatly over the past few years. The traditional part-time cooperative scheme for in-school students, first initiated by Federal legislation in 1936 and requiring fifteen hours a week of on-the-job training, has not proved practical. The 1963 act offers support for full-time pre-employment programs, marking an important step forward in distributive education.

In 1962 the Federal contribution to the program was a modest $2.6 million. State and local funds raised the total program expenditure to $11.4 million.

Trades and industry education. In an industrial society a trades and industry program should be the heart of a well-founded vocational effort to prepare youth for the world of work. Yet the trades and industry program accounts for only 19 percent of the expenditure and 16 percent of the enrollment in the Federal vocational program for in-school youth.

Federal reimbursement supports full-time programs for in-school youth, part-time cooperative programs for in-school youth, special training for apprentices, and extension classes for adult workers. Most of the programs are conducted under the aegis of secondary and post-secondary school institutions, though a few programs do exist in junior colleges. The subject-matter coverage of the program is broadly defined and includes such subjects as food services, carpentry, needle trades, auto repair, fire fighting, printing, tool and die making, sheet metal work, and dry cleaning.

Enrollments in the trades and industry program have remained relatively static over the last two decades, as illustrated in Table 10. At present only one-eighth of the high school students in the large cities of America are enrolled in the program; outside the larger cities the program is

TABLE 10

Enrollment in Vocational Trades and Industry Classes, by Type of Class, 1956–62

(in thousands)

Year	All Classes	Day Classes	Evening Classes	Part-time Classes
1962............	1,005	294	558	153
1961............	964	271	524	168
1960............	938	272	485	181
1959............	968	281	512	175
1958............	984	272	520	191
1957............	952	261	493	197
1956............	884	247	440	197

Source: *Digest of Annual Reports of State Boards of Vocational Education, . . . 1962,* pp. 23, 50. The 1962 enrollments are provisional figures, subject to final review of state reports. Figures may not add to totals because of rounding.

often not available to in-school youth. Nationally, only 2 percent of the fifteen to nineteen age group is enrolled in the program, despite the fact that 30 to 40 percent of this age group must eventually seek employment in an occupation potentially served by the program.

Male enrollment in the trades and industry program is nine times greater than female enrollment. Few programs have been developed in the service occupations, which constitute the most rapidly expanding middle-level occupational area, an area that could be served through the trades and industry program. The program suffers from a continuing lack of qualified teachers. With less than 10 percent of the high schools of the nation offering any trades and industry program, the availability of this form of education remains its most critical drawback.

In 1962 the Federal expenditure for vocational trades and industry education was $11.4 million. The state and local expenditure added $74.6 million to this sum. The total program expenditure in 1962 was only slightly larger than that for the preparation of girls for homemaking. Undoubtedly the Vocational Education Act of 1963 will channel far larger sums into the trades and industry program.

Practical nursing. In 1956 practical nursing was made a part of the Federal vocational education program. The courses, generally twelve months in length, are designed to prepare the student to function in relatively straightforward, patient-centered nursing situations; practical

TABLE 11

Enrollment in the Training Programs for the Health Occupations, by Type of Class, 1956–62

(in thousands)

Year	All Classes	Preparatory Classes	Extension Classes
1962............	58	39	19
1961............	62	37	25
1960............	56	34	22
1959............	38	27	11
1958............	40	23	17
1957............	29	19	10
1956............	28	16	12

Source: *Digest of Annual Reports of State Boards of Vocational Education, . . . 1962,* p. 13.

nurses also serve as operating room assistants, medical and dental assistants, and psychiatric aides. The program is usually conducted through a
hospital or medical center, often with the cooperation of local school
districts or a junior college. Two-thirds of the program enrollees are over
twenty years of age. The extension courses are usually short-unit programs covering nursing specialties. Enrollments in the practical nursing
program have generally continued upward, as shown in Table 11.

The uneven growth of enrollments reflects the growing pains of this
relatively new vocational program. One difficulty is that of gaining recognition of the occupational role of the licensed practical nurse; this corner
seems to have been turned within the medical profession. Another difficulty has been financing; total program expenditure in 1962 was $9.7
million, less than half of which was from Federal sources. The Vocational Education Act of 1963 makes permanent the Federal practical
nursing program.

Office occupations. Training for the office occupations has traditionally
not been reimbursable under Federal vocational legislation; yet this form
of vocational education is offered far more extensively than any other.
The Vocational Education Act of 1963 specifically makes office occupations eligible for support.

Although precise figures are not available, it is estimated that such
programs exist in some 80 percent of the high schools in this country, and
enroll about 1,800,000 students. A significant (but unknown) proportion
of these students, however, are enrolled only for a semester and take the
program for avocational purposes. The secondary schools employ more
than 60,000 business education teachers, compared to 37,000 teachers
engaged in all the federally aided vocational programs. Business education is also one of the most widely taught high school adult education
programs and is by far the most widely taught occupational program of
this country's two-year colleges. In addition, it engages the efforts of
hundreds of post-high-school proprietary schools across the land (see
the section on "Business Schools" in chapter 4).

The extent of offerings is indicative of the growing demand for well-
trained workers in the office occupations. During this decade, as indicated earlier, the number of employment opportunities in this field is
expected to increase by 27 percent, or nearly 3 million new jobs. In addition, 400,000 new workers are needed annually as replacements in this

high turnover field. Increasing use of electronic office equipment and the expansion of secretarial opportunities in scientific, engineering, medical, and other special fields will require a higher level of education and skill for many of the new entrants into the office and secretarial occupations. Good secretaries and specialty secretaries especially are already in short supply in almost all parts of the country. The need is not only for more, but also for more specialized, programs in these occupations.

Area vocational education. The area vocational program is a product of title VIII of the National Defense Education Act. In passing this legislation, Congress took recognition of the acute shortage of science and engineering technicians, the shortage of training facilities for them, and the inability of most smaller communities and single school districts to set up such facilities. Accordingly, title VIII offers aid to "area schools" (those admitting students from more than one school district) offering courses to train highly skilled technicians in occupations necessary to the national defense.

Under U.S. Office of Education "area school" definitions, any multi-district public institution may offer a federally reimbursable program, at *any* level from the eleventh through the fifteenth grades. In 1962 the number of schools offering highly skilled technician training was over 600, with more than 1,000 preparatory courses and 1,500 extension courses being taught (Table 12). Although numbering only a fifth of the total schools involved, the junior-community colleges now enroll 40 percent of all students in the program. Over-all program enrollments have risen sharply in each of the past five years (Table 13), but are still far short of meeting the estimated yearly demand for 100,000 new science and engineering technicians.

The need to expand technician training programs is obvious. The expansion of present programs and creation of new ones is severely hampered by the desperate shortage of qualified teachers. This problem—common among vocational programs—is especially acute because competent technical personnel can command higher pay in industry than many schools can afford. Another difficulty is the weak financing: in 1963 the program expenditure was only $32 million, of which $15 million came from Federal sources.

Two arbitrary measures of the progress of an educational program are enrollment and finance. By either of these measures, the federally supported program of vocational education has been losing ground. Again, however, these figures do not reflect passage of the Vocational Education Act of 1963.

TABLE 12

Number of Institutions Offering NDEA Title VIII Programs, by Type, 1959–62

Institution	1959	1960	1961	1962
Comprehensive high school........	73	153	168	193
Vocational-technical high school...	..	44	66	125
Technical high school.............	14	17	49	43
Vocational or trade school.........	86	126	106	74
Technical institute................	17	52	25	27
Community or junior college.......	38	119	126	129
Four-year college.................	10	16	17	26
State schools.....................	20	2	13	13
Other............................	4	8	..	..

Source: Division of Vocational and Technical Education, U.S. Office of Education, *Progress in Title VIII Programs, Fiscal Year 1962* (Mimeographed; Washington: The Office, March 1963), p. 2. The 1962 figures are provisional, subject to final audit of state reports.

TABLE 13

Enrollment in Area Vocational Education Programs, by Type of Class, 1959–63

(in thousands)

Year	Total	Preparatory Classes		Extension Classes
		High School	Postsecondary	
1963............	168	15	50	103
1962............	149	13	40	96
1961............	123	12	27	84
1960............	101	7	26	68
1959............	49	(N.A.)	19	29

Source: *Progress in Title VIII Programs, Fiscal Year 1962*, p. 1. Figures for 1963 are estimated. Figures may not add to totals because of rounding.

Enrollment: a summary. The decade 1950–60 saw a 50 percent increase in secondary school attendance in the United States. During this same period enrollment in vocational agriculture, distributive occupations, home economics, and trades and industry classes showed less than

8 percent increase. When enrollees in the new practical nursing (1956) and area vocational education (1958) programs are added, an increase of 10.7 percent is recorded. Vocational classes have been enrolling a dwindling proportion of school-age youth.

That nearly 4 million persons are enrolled in all categories of the federally supported vocational and technical education program would seem to indicate a healthy condition. An analysis of the figure, however, gives little encouragement to those who believe that in a technological society occupational education should be a legitimate and necessary form of education, one that will provide young adults with a bridge between school and work and provide the nation with necessary resources of skilled manpower.

In 1962 about 55 percent of these 4 million were people beyond high school age registered in evening or part-time classes. Only 45 percent of the 4 million (about 1.8 million) were attending day classes; almost all of these people were in high school or postsecondary schools. But of the full-time students, 56 percent (largely girls) were in vocational home economics courses designed to prepare students for homemaking, and *not* payroll jobs. There remained about 830,000 high school students (475,000 in agriculture, 295,000 in trades and industry, 45,000 in distributive occupations, 15,000 in area vocational programs, a handful in practical nursing) who were enrolled on a reasonably full-time basis in pre-employment training programs during 1962. The great majority of these youth are in the fourteen to seventeen age group, 13.5 million of whom were enrolled in public high schools in the 1962–63 school year. *Thus, the federally aided program in secondary schools is providing full-time pre-employment training for a bare 6 percent of the age group it is designed to serve.*

Moreover, the 830,000 students receiving full-time, pre-employment training in secondary schools are largely spread throughout grades nine through twelve. How many enrollees graduate from the vocational programs is not known. It is known, however, that dropout and transfer from the program are high, particularly in the large cities and in the South. A substantial proportion of the 830,000, then, are in the ninth and tenth grades. An educated guess is that no more than 4 or 5 percent of the high school graduates in any one year are persons completing a full-time, pre-employment curriculum which receives Federal financial aid.

A further breakdown of these 830,000 students shows that about 57 percent are enrolled in vocational agriculture. Agriculture now accounts for only 8 percent of all employment; yet the vocational agriculture enrollment has increased 36 percent since 1940. Conversely, only 35 percent of the Federal program enrollees are in the trades and industry programs. This enrollment has increased only 23 percent since 1940, an increase largely accounted for by a 79 percent increase in enrollments in the South. It is unfortunate for the students and the needs of the country that the trades and industry program, meager enough before World War II, has shown a decline in enrollments in many of the most industrialized areas in the country.

All occupational education does not, of course, take place within the federally aided program: a certain number of school systems have decided to establish independent vocational programs, as have a very small number of private and parochial secondary schools. And a certain percentage of all high school graduates will be able to find post-high-school occupational education available to them. But few high school students receive an education for the world of work they are about to enter.

Finance: a summary. The pattern of Federal financial assistance to vocational education is indicated by Table 14. In the decade 1950–60,

TABLE 14

Total Expenditure for Vocational Education, by Type of Program, 1956–62

(in thousands)

Year	Total	Agriculture	Distributive Occupations	Home Economics	Trades and Industry	Practical Nursing	Area Vocational
1962...	$283,948	$73,292	$11,406	$79,898	$85,087	$9,660	$24,606
1961...	254,073	69,607	10,593	72,622	75,396	7,450	18,406
1960...	238,812	67,302	9,900	68,656	72,860	6,067	14,027
1959...	228,315	66,668	9,602	67,001	73,504	4,721	6,819
1958...	209,748	64,542	9,303	62,910	69,423	3,570	....
1957...	190,726	59,915	8,173	57,178	64,075	1,386	....
1956...	175,886	56,658	6,424	53,282	59,522	......	....

Source: *Digest of Annual Reports of State Boards of Vocational Education, . . . 1962,* p. 28. Figures may not add to totals because of rounding.

the increase in Federal expenditures for vocational education amounted to $19 million, a 70 percent increase. During this same period the increase in state and local expenditures amounted to $91 million, a 90 percent increase. The Federal contribution, through 1963, represented a diminishing portion of the total program expenditure. In 1961 the Federal expenditure represented 19 percent of the total program expenditure.

The total program expenditure increased by 87 percent during the 1950's. By way of contrast, the national expenditure for public elementary and secondary education increased 167 percent during this same period. Stated thus, vocational education has been getting a progressively smaller portion of the national expenditure on education.

POSTSECONDARY OCCUPATIONAL EDUCATION

Opportunities for postsecondary occupational education are best described as a sometime thing. The variety of institutions that offer programs, the wide range of approaches among the various states, and the resulting disparity of opportunity open to students in various parts of the country, all serve to make definitions and generalizations virtually impossible. However, this is an area of education upon which the new technology has placed the stamp of utmost importance, an area ripe for new thinking and vigorous leadership.

This report has underscored the importance of greatly expanding and improving the occupational education effort of the high schools. For many students and many occupations, the high school must be the focal point of effort. But a *total* occupational education effort—one giving recognition to the full range of student abilities, aptitudes, and interests and to the full range of skill and educational requisites of a changing occupational spectrum—demands that much of this education be offered at the post-high-school level.

The sections that follow will outline the post-high-school occupational education opportunities in the United States today.

No single pattern.   There is no single pattern of institutional responsibility for occupational education beyond the high school in the various states. Programs of every kind and quality are offered by a variety of educational institutions, including comprehensive high schools, trade and technical high schools, area vocational schools, technical institutes, special state schools, two-year colleges, four-year colleges, and universities. A recent U.S. Office of Education survey listed forty-eight different institutional titles of publicly supported schools working in this field. At least three distinct administrative approaches are identifiable: (1) the program may be administered at the local or community level, for example, within one or more school districts, or within a city, county, or specially created two-year college district; (2) all programs within a state may be administered by a designated state board; (3) programs may be conducted under the aegis of the state university as part of the state's plan for higher education. The first and second approaches, or some combination of the two, are the most prevalent; institutionally, they have lent themselves to the development of area vocational schools and comprehensive two-year colleges.

A variety of approaches is used to finance these programs. Federal funds are available to certain programs and certain institutions, but not to others; at that, by the time Federal funds are apportioned to the local level, they may amount to only 5 or 10 percent of the program cost. The money, then, must come from local or state governments, tuition charges, or some combination of the three, each a very limited source. In almost all of the states studied, serious problems of finance stood in the way of expanding and improving occupational education opportunities. Most states see the need for greatly enlarged efforts, but they have been unable to find sources of revenue to support program expansion.

Tuition and entry requirements vary throughout the nation. Tuition charges in some two-year colleges run to $500 a year and more; in most area schools and in the California junior college system, however, there are no tuition charges, and other fees, if any, are nominal. For many youth, tuition determines opportunity or lack of opportunity for post-high-school occupational education.

Entrance requirements, too, affect opportunity. In some states and schools, high school graduation or its equivalent or even a minimum age (such as eighteen) and a willingness to attend are sufficient for admission. In other places, deliberate policy or limitation of space restricts admission to those with high rank in their graduating class, with high scores on certain tests, or with certain course prerequisites. Racial exclusions of various kinds exist in many states.

Notwithstanding these factors, the greatest single barrier to post-high-school occupational education opportunities is their physical unavailability: a substantial majority of the people in this country will not find an appropriate institution within commuting distance of their residence.

The area school.   Area vocational education has already been mentioned in the discussion of high school vocational and technical education. Although area schools are usually operated as an adjunct of secondary education, a significant part of their work is at the post-high-school level. A relatively recent phenomenon in American education, they perform a variety of functions that do not lend themselves to easy classification within the traditional ladder of American education. In a given area school, for example, the morning hours may be given over to vocational training for high school students who are brought by bus from several surrounding high schools. In the afternoon the school's facilities may be used by trainees enrolled under the Manpower Development and Training Act or the Area Redevelopment Act. On into the night, the classrooms and shops may be filled with adults taking extension courses.

The courses taught during the day will have ranged from the most straightforward craft to a quite sophisticated technical skill; the school will have served the in-school youth, the unemployed teen-ager or adult, the worker seeking to update or upgrade his skill; some area schools report schedules of eighteen hours a day. In effect, these are ungraded schools. They now number more than 300, and are spread over some 38 states. Their popularity is signaled by their burgeoning enrollments (an estimated 500,000 in 1963), by waiting lists for admission, and by plans to construct another 100 schools in the immediate future. But again, 300 or even 400 such schools are too few in a country as large as the United States, especially when the majority are concentrated in eight to ten states, most of which are in the South or Midwest.

The area schools are highly specialized, single-purpose institutions. General education is often nonexistent in their programs. Most of them are modern and well equipped. They have a no-nonsense atmosphere about them. Educationally, they have certain drawbacks, but the urgent individual and national demand for the skills these schools provide and the occupational education foot-dragging of more comprehensive educational institutions seems to augur a further reliance on the area school approach in many states.

The two-year college.   There were in 1963 more than 700 two-year colleges in the United States. Of these, 470 were public, 238 private; every state but one can claim at least one such school. Opening fall enrollment in 1963 was 847,572, almost equally divided between full-time and part-time students. These figures include locally controlled junior (or community) colleges, state junior colleges, private junior colleges, technical institutes and semiprofessional schools, and branches or extension centers of four-year colleges and universities offering a two-year program. The enrollment figures include 34 institutions with more than 5,000 students enrolled and 107 with fewer than 100 enrolled.

The comprehensive junior, or community, college has come a long way over the six decades of its existence. Its early lower-division, college-parallel function has now been broadened to encompass a scope of purpose aptly described by the Michigan Council of Community College Administrators:

> A community college is a locally controlled, public, two-year institution of higher education which offers broad, comprehensive programs of instruction for persons of post-high-school age.
> A community college expands opportunities for education beyond the high school by (1) offering programs in occupational, technical, and semi-professional training for students planning to enter a vocation as well as the first and second year college academic courses for students planning to transfer to four-year colleges or universities, (2) adhering to an "open door" general admission policy but being selective in those whom it retains, graduates and recommends for placement, (3) responding to the particular educational needs of the community it serves, (4) drawing upon its community's total resources in organizing its instructional programs, (5) enrolling students on a full or part-time basis, and (6) offering day and evening classes and programs of instruction, and, if economically feasible, on a year-round basis.[1]

Taken as a whole, American junior colleges do not give proper attention to the occupational education phase of their purpose. Less than a quarter of all junior college students are enrolled in organized occupational curricula. In 1960, the most recent year for which comprehensive figures are available, 170,831 students were enrolled in such curricula in two-year colleges, a gain of 47,000 students over 1957 figures. Of these, 59,004 were in engineering-related curricula, and 111,827 in nonengineering-related curricula; 1960 graduates from the former category numbered 10,190, and from the latter 22,958.[2]

---

[1] Quoted in Harold T. Smith, *Education and Training for the World of Work* (Kalamazoo, Mich.: W. E. Upjohn Institute for Employment Research, 1963), p. 4.

[2] Ken August Brunner, "The Training of Subprofessional Personnel in the United States," Paper prepared for the International Conference on Middle Level Manpower, San Juan, Puerto Rico, Oct. 10–12, 1962 (Mimeographed), pp. 24, 32.

Large gaps appear in the availability of occupational curricula in the two-year college: a count reveals California with 334, but seven states with none. Moreover, over half the enrollees are in two states—California and New York; Pennsylvania, Illinois, and Michigan account for another 20 percent of the enrollees.[3]

A growing number of reports, many of them carefully considered, point to the comprehensive two-year college as the logical vehicle for post-high-school occupational education. The prolonged failure of the two-year college to "run with the ball" has, however, raised the question whether the two-year college will truly meet the needs of youth seeking occupational education opportunities beyond the high school. Leland L. Medsker, a sympathetic but perceptive observer of the junior college movement, states that:

> It is obvious from the data presented that the two-year college in America is focused more on the transfer than the terminal function. If, then, the institution is adjudged unique solely on the basis of its special services to students who do not transfer, it fails to measure up.[4]

The reasons for emphasis on the transfer function are many, including the relatively greater expense of conducting occupational curricula, the difficulty of recruiting competent teachers, a lack of understanding on the part of students and parents, and the greater prestige and status of offering a college liberal arts program. These factors must be overcome, and it will take more than the wishing of concerned educators to do the job. Indeed, the failure of the two-year college to assume the major responsibility for occupational education beyond the high school will mean that this necessary societal function will be performed through educationally less desirable avenues, such as area skill centers or Federal crash programs of manpower training. This has, in fact, already begun to occur.

Let us now examine two contrasting state two-year college systems.

California is our most populous state, and it has the largest college enrollment (718,480 in 1963) in the nation. Its per-capita expenditure for public education at all levels is one of the highest in the nation.

---

[3] Computed from U.S. Office of Education, *Total Enrollment in Institutions of Higher Education, First Term, 1959–60* (Washington: Government Printing Office, 1962).

[4] Medsker, *The Junior College: Progress and Prospect* (New York: McGraw-Hill Book Co., 1960), p. 112.

Unique among systems of higher education is California's policy of free tuition in public junior colleges for all residents.

The system in the fall of 1963 included the seven-campus University of California, 16 four-year colleges, and 68 two-year colleges. Admissions are governed by a systemwide policy. High school graduates in the top 12.5 percent of their class are eligible to enroll at the state university; those in the top 33.3 percent are admitted to the state four-year colleges. Admission to the public junior colleges is liberal, requiring graduation from high school or its equivalent, or eighteen years of age plus permission. This admission policy and that of free tuition has led to the enrollment of one of the largest proportions of high school graduates in post-high-school education in the nation. The state plans to expand its junior college system to put such an institution within commuting distance of all citizens within a few years.

Public support of the local junior college is based on a property tax levied within a designated junior college taxing district. Direct state aid is also provided, now amounting to about one-quarter of the operating costs of the junior college. Although the junior colleges currently are having financial difficulties in the face of limited state funds, the combination of sources of revenue provided by law assures them of a reasonably long-term, secure financial footing, a crucial item in their development.

Almost all California junior colleges offer occupational and college-transfer programs. In some of the larger junior colleges, such as Fullerton Junior College, Los Angeles Trade-Technical College, Modesto Junior College, and Oakland City, San Diego City, and San Francisco City Colleges, thirty or more different occupational curricula are offered, usually encompassing the applied and graphic arts, business and commerce, agriculture, horticulture and forestry, the skilled trades and crafts, the science and engineering technologies, and health, government, recreation, and other services. In October 1962 about one-third of the 354,341 full- and part-time students in the state's junior colleges were enrolled in occupationally oriented courses.

New York has the second largest number of two-year colleges in the country. The approach of New York is in many respects different from that of California. While California is attempting to meet educational needs beyond the high school with a system of tuition-free, publicly supported two-year colleges, post-high-school education policy in New York is influenced by private institutions and a lesser number of public institutions that charge substantial tuition fees. Comprehensive plans for occupational and higher education will alter the picture to some degree, but New York will still offer a sharp contrast to California.

Both vocational and technical education have fared poorly in New York in the past. Post-high-school occupational education has historically been a function of secondary education in the cities and of a half-dozen agricultural-industrial-technical institutes in other parts of the state. Even today, Texas counts twice as many enrollees in her federally supported vocational and technical programs as does New York.

In 1948 a general reorganization of public higher education in New York led to the creation of the State University of New York. The two-year institutes were made a part of the State University system, and, under permissive legislation, a few of them have evolved into comprehensive two-year community colleges. The 1948 reorganization also permitted local governmental jurisdictions to set up two-year community colleges under the supervision of the State University and the Board of Regents; 21 such institutions have been founded since 1948, and now enroll 30,000 students. Few of these new institutions, however, are "comprehensive" in the sense of offering occupational as well as transfer programs, and the transfer function still dominates the programs of the private two-year colleges. All told, the 27 public and 25 private two-year colleges in New York enrolled some 62,000 students in 1962.

The lack of emphasis on terminal-occupational programs in higher education in New York stands in contrast to the California approach. Under a plan recently submitted to the New York State Legislature by the State Education Department, both secondary and postsecondary industrial and technical training needs would be provided through a state-wide system of area skill centers. New York, under this proposal, would follow the pattern of several Southern and Midwestern states and make occupational education a special and separate form of secondary education rather than an integral part of a comprehensive scheme of higher education. This plan has been furthered to some degree by the failure of institutions of higher education in New York generally to accept occupational education as a part of their responsibility.

The state's comprehensive community colleges do, of course, offer some occupational education. They contrast with their counterparts in California in their more rigid admission requirements and substantial tuition charges. Since they each depend on student fees for about a third of their operating costs, tuition levels are among the highest in public higher education. The state has, however, a generous scholarship and loan program, which extends opportunity to many students.

Other states show varying approaches and degrees of effort. *Wisconsin* has a system of junior colleges; yet they are prohibited from offering vocational and technical programs, which are left to 61 separately administered schools of the area type spread over the state. Other states, such as *Iowa,* are planning a state-wide system of public two-year colleges, whose comprehensive programs will include occupational curricula. *North Carolina* has worked hard to establish a system of area industrial education centers, and in 1963 passed legislation permitting their evolution into comprehensive junior colleges. On the other hand, a few Eastern states, such as *New Jersey* and *Massachusetts,* have done little to provide occupational education.

The technical institute. Traditionally, the technical institute has provided the leadership for technical education in this country. Although its efforts are now overshadowed by the work of the two- and four-year colleges and the area school, it remains a substantial source of education for highly skilled science and engineering technicians.

Technical institutes have been particularly identified with curricula in the engineering technologies, and have long enjoyed close relationships with the engineering profession. They are generally single-purpose, post-high-school institutions, with programs averaging two years in length. Many of them have been privately endowed or proprietary institutions, with sizable tuition and fees, selective admissions policies, and rigorous programs of study.

A count of technical institutes has become difficult in recent years. The schools that are technical institutes *only* probably number no more than four or five dozen. But over the last twenty years a variety of other institutions have undertaken to offer curricula of the technical institute *type.* These other institutions include two-year colleges, four-year colleges and universities, comprehensive vocational-technical schools, and area schools. A discriminating count by Henninger, made in 1957, found 144 institutions offering curricula considered to be of "technical institute character"; of these, 92 were public and 52 private.[5]

[5] G. Ross Henninger, *The Technical Institute in America* (New York: McGraw-Hill Book Co., 1959), p. 4.

With the passage of title VIII of the National Defense Education Act in 1958, however, the number of institutions offering technical education curricula (in the science and engineering technologies) has skyrocketed. In 1959, 262 institutions, all public, participated in the federally assisted program; by 1962 the number had risen to 630. (How many of their curricula would qualify as "technical institute" in type is another matter.) During this period the number of public two- and four-year colleges and technical institutes participating rose from 65 to 182, an indication that Henninger's count would have to be raised considerably today. Although enrollment counts are equally precarious, a rough estimate would place the number of full-time students in the technical institute type of curriculum at 40,000 to 50,000, with about 15,000 graduates a year.

Accreditation of the technical institute type of curriculum was initiated in 1944 by the Engineers' Council for Professional Development. In 1955 the ECPD accredited programs in 30 institutions; yet in 1963 only 33 institutions had accredited programs.[6] One of the major issues in technical education is this ECPD-accrediting effort. Although regional accrediting agencies in the nation have operated on the principle of accrediting the institution, the ECPD has adopted the principle of accrediting individual curricula. Some institutions have resisted this approach. Others have ignored it since employers do not seem to care whether or not the technician comes from an accredited program. This has sharply limited the number of ECPD-accredited curricula; in 1955 there were 93, in 1963 there were 126. Probably there are many more having a technical institute type of curriculum which could meet ECPD approval if it were sought.

General education receives little attention in most of these curricula. As separate, single-purpose, highly specialized institutions, the original technical schools saw their goal as the most thorough possible preparation of the student in his chosen field of technology, and these schools did not believe a two-year curriculum left time for general studies. Moreover, as separate schools, many did not have the staff or academic facilities to include any substantial general education content in their curriculum. This situation continues today in many curricula of the technical institute type, especially in the independent institutes. A study of 48 institutes made in 1954 revealed that in ECPD-accredited cur-

[6] Engineers' Council for Professional Development, *30th Annual Report for the Year Ending September 30, 1962* (New York: The Council, 1962), p. 49.

ricula an average of 9.6 percent of the total time (contact hours) was given over to general education; in non-ECPD–accredited curricula the percentage was 5.51.[7] The same ratios would probably apply today to the ECPD-accredited curricula. Among the nonaccredited curricula, however, the same ratio would probably not maintain since many of the newer programs of the two- and four-year colleges display an increase of general education content. Those responsible for such programs have reached no agreement about the optimum ratio of special to general.

Henninger concluded that the non-tax-supported technical institute has provided leadership and gives continuity to the "technical institute idea." Hopefully, these schools will continue their leadership and experimentation, although it now appears that the comprehensive two-year college will be the principal institutional home of the technical curricula.

Colleges and universities. Occupational education is no stranger to colleges and universities. James F. Davidson suggests that the classical curriculum of the early American college was, in a sense, vocational: it prepared students to become men of the world, which was their particular vocation, and enough of that world was recognizable in Greek and Latin texts to make them a useful and practical means of education.[8] The land-grant colleges introduced the immediately vocational into higher education; their work during their first two or three decades was much like that of a comprehensive high school today. Over the years occupational curricula have been devised for law, medicine, engineering, teaching, business, agriculture, home economics, journalism, and many other occupations, whether or not they constitute "professions." There are today only a handful of colleges that do not offer occupationally oriented curricula on the baccalaureate level. A striking note is how much is being done on the four-year level and how little is being done on the one- to three-year levels.

In 1959, 403 four-year colleges and universities were offering occupational curricula of subbaccalaureate level.[9] No clear pattern emerges

---

[7] Edward E. Booker, "Survey of General Education in Technical Institutes," *Technical Education News*, XIV, special issue 1954, 6. Study also presented in Henninger, *The Technical Institute in America*, pp. 44–46.

[8] Davidson, "On Furniture, First Jobs, and Freedom," *Liberal Education*, XLIX (May 1963), 268.

[9] Brunner, "The Training of Subprofessional Personnel in the United States," p. 12.

in the type of institution that has entered this field; the 403 schools range from large state universities to small private institutions which regard themselves as "pure" liberal arts colleges.

In October 1960, 75,665 students were enrolled in subbaccalaureate occupational curricula in four-year institutions; 44,014 were full-time students, 31,651 part-time.[10] The average number of these students per institution was 188, an indication that many institutions have small enrollments in their programs. In 1960, 18,732 students graduated from these programs, 5,697 from engineering-related curricula, 13,035 from other fields.[11] Although recent figures are not available, data for the late 1950's indicate that an increasing percentage of the subbaccalaureate occupational curricula are being offered in the two-year colleges. In 1956, for example, 44 percent of the enrollees in such curricula were in four-year institutions; by 1960 about 30 percent were.[12] Brunner concludes:

> First, it appears that the higher educational institutions can be expected to provide at least one-fourth and perhaps as much as one-third of the sub-professional personnel needed. Second, the happiest institution for such programs is increasingly the community or junior college. Apparently the 2-year institution is more able than the 4-year colleges and universities to attract students to sub-professional programs and hold them for the two years needed to complete such preparation. Besides, the status factor of the bachelor's degree is less a problem in an institution which does not award bachelor's degrees. Third, unless higher education institutions accept a much greater responsibility for this level of education than they have in recent years, and at a much more rapid rate, the largest proportion of the needs for sub-professional personnel will have to be satisfied by other kinds of education and training.[13]

The Pennsylvania State University is an excellent example of the work of a major university in subbaccalaureate occupational education. The university offers two-year curricula leading to the associate degree in agriculture, hotel and food service, drafting and design technology, electrical technology, production technology, surveying technology, business administration, chemical technology, and metallurgical technology. Programs are offered on the main campus and at thirteen other

[10] *Ibid.,* p. 18.
[11] *Loc. cit.*
[12] *Ibid.,* p. 19.
[13] *Ibid.,* pp. 34–35.

locations in the state for graduates of accredited secondary schools. Most of Penn State's associate degree program is currently concentrated in the engineering technologies. Students participate in the normal university program of student activities and services; counseling, orientation, and placement services are also available. Enrollment in subbaccalaureate programs in the fall of 1959 was 4,575 students.

Similar programs are offered in Indiana by Purdue University (2,007 students in 1959) and in Oklahoma by Oklahoma State University (1,265 students in terminal occupational programs in 1959). At least two dozen other four-year institutions are currently making a substantial effort, having terminal occupational programs enrolling 500 students or more.

4. Other Opportunities for Vocational and Technical Education

WITHIN CERTAIN LIMITATIONS, organized occupational curricula in formal secondary and higher education provide a substantial number of opportunities related to the world of work. In addition, however, there are many other sources of occupational preparation and upgrading in this country. This chapter will consider a few of the more important sources, most of which come under the general heading of "continuing education."

The importance of continuing education in a technological society has been underscored at several points in this report. Yet the public institutions of secondary and higher education in the United States as a whole have not demonstrated an appropriate commitment to this area. A principal exception to this rule is the field of vocational and technical education, whose leaders have long recognized the importance of continuing education and who have, with limited public understanding and financial support, made great efforts in this area. But even these efforts have fallen considerably short of the needs for continuing occupational education.

An excellent picture of the scope of continuing education is presented by a recent study conducted by the National Opinion Research Center and sponsored by the Carnegie Corporation of New York. Information on the first phase of the study has recently been released under the title *Volunteers for Learning: A Study of Educational Pursuits of American Adults,* by John W. C. Johnstone.[1] It reports on the prospects of those over twenty-one who seek to gain knowledge, information, or skill in

[1] National Opinion Research Center Report No. 89 (Chicago: The Center, 1963). Excellent summaries of the study appear in *Facts and Figures on Adult Education,* Vol. I, No. 1 (April 1963), issued by Division of Adult Education Service, N.E.A., and in *Continuing Education for Adults,* No. 32, March 1963, issued by Center for the Study of Liberal Education for Adults.

an organized instruction program at any level and in any place. The study estimated that in the period June 1, 1961, to June 1, 1962, 2,650,000 full-time and 17,160,000 part-time adult students enrolled in various educational programs, and 8,960,000 adults engaged in self-education.

Adult education offerings, according to the report, showed the following characteristics: (1) The post-high-school educational energies of American adults are directed primarily to vocational and recreational concerns. (2) The fields of general education, religion, and home and family life each claim about one-eighth of the total activities, while all other categories have a relatively minor impact on the over-all patterns. (3) Together colleges and universities and elementary and secondary schools sponsored only one-third of the courses reported.

Programs of continuing education are offered in many places. The adults in programs cited by the study were distributed as follows: churches and synagogues, 3,460,000; colleges and universities, 3,440,-000; community organizations, 2,450,000; business and industry, 2,040,000; elementary and secondary schools, 1,920,000; private schools, 1,220,000; government, 1,180,000; the Armed Forces, 580,000. Fewer than half the courses reported were sponsored by institutions whose primary function is education.

The study reported that the level of previous educational attainment was the biggest single factor influencing participation in adult education programs (see Table 15). Occupation and income influence participation rates in continuing education, but the influence is minor compared to that of educational level achieved in formal schooling.

TABLE 15

Rates of Participation in Adult Education, by Previous Educational Attainment, Occupation, and Family Income

(percent who studied any subject by any method)

OCCUPATION	GRADE SCHOOL			HIGH SCHOOL			COLLEGE		
	Under $4,000	$4,000–$6,999	$7,000 over	Under $4,000	$4,000 $6,999	$7,000 over	Under $4,000	$4,000–$6,999	$7,000 over
Blue collar...	7	8	11	20	21	23	37	40	37
White collar..	9	11	14	22	21	29	37	45	43

Source: *Continuing Education for Adults,* No. 32 (Chicago: Center for the Study of Liberal Education for Adults, March 1963), p. 5.

The report concludes that the more education one has, the more likely one will engage in additional learning experiences. It becomes obvious from this study that the vast pool of untrained, undereducated, and unemployed persons in the nation is not being reached through present continuing education programs. The closest source of such programs for most people would be the public schools.

CONTINUING EDUCATION IN THE PUBLIC SCHOOLS

Educational programs for adults are offered by many public schools throughout the nation. The most relevant report available is a study of the United States Office of Education of the 1958–59 school year.[2] The definition of adult education on which these data are based is those organized public educational programs (excluding regular full-time school programs) whose primary purpose is the development of skills, knowledge, habits, or attitudes through formal instruction of an organized nature. It excludes activities that are primarily social, recreational, or goods-producing and those that are offered by junior colleges, institutes, or any other institutions of higher education.

The report estimated that total enrollment during the 1958–59 school year was 3.4 million. However, since many persons enrolled for more than one course, the number of individuals was estimated to be 2.9 million. During the year 1958–59, 4,840 of the 15,200 school districts in the country offered an adult education program. Approximately 4,420 adults graduated from elementary schools and 21,300 from high schools through such programs.

Five fields of instruction accounted for over two-thirds of the 135,000 classes offered during the year. These fields were, by number of classes: trades, industrial, and technical courses, 27,300; homemaking and consumer education, 20,400; high school academic education, 15,900; business education, 14,600; and techniques in practical arts and crafts, 12,500.

Funds used for the adult education program amounted to $76.4 million for the school year. Approximately 41 percent came from local tax sources, 20 percent from fees, 18 percent from state aid, 17 percent from Federal aid for vocational education, and 6 percent from other

[2] U.S. Office of Education, *Statistics of Public School Adult Education, 1958–59* (Washington: Government Printing Office, 1961).

sources. The average amount of funds spent in school systems having adult programs was $15,800, but the median was only $1,290. Clearly, only a negligible effort is made in the vast majority of the school systems in the United States. The data also indicate that the larger school systems depend much less on fees or tuition than do smaller school systems. A wide divergence in the quality and variety of offerings is suggested by the study's report that average enrollment per school district in such programs was 710, while the median enrollment was 80. It must be assumed, therefore, that a majority of the schools reporting offered only a very small program for adults.

A good estimate would be that the public school systems of the United States enrolled about 1.5 million adults in courses related to the world of work. Most of the enrollees are in vocational or technical education courses that are a part of the Federal program, and the previously outlined limitations of that program, particularly with respect to the narrow range of courses offered and their restricted availability, apply with equal force to adult education offerings. Time, energy, funds, and a sense of urgency have all been lacking in the public school vocational and technical programs for youth and adults. The adult enrollment in the program represents a little more than 2 percent of the total labor force. To cite this statistic is to note the inadequacy of the present effort.

HIGHER EDUCATION

The Johnstone study estimates that college and university-sponsored adult education programs enrolled 2,640,000 different persons during the sample year studied. Vocational subjects are reported to account for 39 percent of the extension courses sponsored by higher education. If we assume that all courses were equally attended, it can be projected that some 1 million adults were enrolled in vocational subjects in higher education.

In considering vocational and technical education, however, these figures can be quite misleading. The National Opinion Research Center "vocational subjects" classification includes many subjects of an avocational nature. Moreover, a very large portion of the projected 1 million adults were undoubtedly enrolled in short-term extension courses that bear little relationship to the vocational- or technical-level occupations;

teachers, businessmen, farmers, engineers, and not craftsmen or technicians, are the clientele most frequently served. In 1962, for example, the 182 technical institutes, two-year colleges, and four-year colleges and universities participating in the title VIII technical education program enrolled only 46,000 adults in their extension programs. Brunner reports that the total part-time enrollment in all subbaccalaureate occupational curricula in higher education was 83,584 students in October 1960.[3] These enrollments represent an effort far short of the needs for occupational education. The generalizations made earlier about subbaccalaureate occupational education programs in higher education apply with equal force to the extension activities of those programs.

Just as occupational education itself is no stranger to higher education, adult education through extension programs is also a function familiar to this nation's colleges and universities. One of the best examples, of course, is the Cooperative Agricultural Extension Service, a long-established, highly successful adjunct of public higher education offered by land-grant institutions in every part of the country. Altogether there are nearly 800,000 adults served through various continuing education programs in higher education. An Office of Education survey of 1959–60 enrollments showed 234,571 in extension degree-credit courses, 100,542 in correspondence courses, and 3,917 in radio-TV degree-credit courses, 277,462 in non-degree-credit adult general education courses, 66,336 in correspondence non-degree-credit courses, 155,769 in short courses, and 29,406 taking individual lessons.[4] University of Wisconsin President Fred H. Harrington recently testified that

> as a philosophy, university extension sees the campus as a community of scholars making itself as useful as possible to the total society from which the institution draws its inspiration and support. As a function, university extension seeks to identify public problems and public needs, to interpret these concerns to the university, to focus university skills and resources upon them, and thence to translate university insights into educational programs throughout the state or region. It represents work of college grade, though not necessarily carrying college credit. Some of it, for example, is at the post-doctoral level and some includes

[3] Ken August Brunner, "The Training of Subprofessional Personnel in the United States," Paper prepared for the International Conference on Middle Level Manpower, San Juan, Puerto Rico (Mimeographed; Washington, 1962), p. 18.

[4] U.S. Office of Education, *Total Enrollment in Institutions of Higher Education, First Term, 1959–60* (Washington: Government Printing Office, 1962), p. 2.

a wide variety of subject matter not specifically paralleled by any campus course.[5]

Despite the strides being made by the extension program, there remains a dearth of continuing occupational education opportunities on the highly skilled and technical level in higher education. The resultant denial of occupational opportunity to individuals and loss of skilled manpower to the nation has led to a variety of other approaches to the problem of keeping people employable and jobs filled, approaches often educationally less desirable.

BUSINESS AND INDUSTRY

There are many reasons to expect that business and industry would be very much involved in educational and training activities. Indeed, one study estimated that the activity of business and industry was greater than that of all the colleges and universities combined.[6] Nonetheless, it must be understood what these activities entail and what they do not entail. Three recent studies shed light on this subject.

In 1961 the American Council on Education published *Educational Activities of Business,* by Oscar N. Serbein.[7] The report indicated that major in-company educational programs may generally be placed in two categories—supervisory executive training and professional or technical training. The first is aimed at improving managerial capacity at the top middle-management levels; the second is designed to improve technical competence *at the professional level.* Serbein reports that of 300 large (over 10,000 employees) firms studied, only 8 percent included hourly workers among those eligible for company training programs. Of 228 smaller firms surveyed, only 6 percent reported that all employees were eligible for courses. Serbein also reports on out-of-company programs involving cooperation with educational institutions. Of 212 large industrial firms surveyed, only 52 percent acknowledged that all employees were eligible; but even in these firms, opportunity was often

[5] From a statement on H.R. 3000, 88th Cong., 1st Sess., June 12, 1963 (Mimeographed), p. 7.

[6] Harold F. Clark and Harold S. Sloan, *Classrooms in the Factories* (Rutherford, N.J.: Fairleigh Dickinson University, 1958).

[7] Serbein, *Educational Activities of Business* (Washington: American Council on Education, 1961).

restricted to higher echelon personnel by the nature of the courses offered and the educational requisites for participation in them.

A 1962 Department of Labor survey presents a similar picture.[8] The survey covered 710,662 establishments in the United States, employing from four to over 500 employees each. In the spring of 1962, 136,659 establishments had training programs in operation; this segment represented 19.2 percent of all establishments and 48.1 percent of all workers (some 36 million persons in all) included in the survey. At that particular time only 7.1 percent of all employees covered by the survey were actually being trained. The survey revealed that opportunities for company training varied from industry to industry, with the percentage of employees involved in training ranging from 13.8 percent in retail trade to 2.5 percent in the category comprising transportation, communication, and public utilities; manufacturing stood at 6.0 percent. Size of business also was an important factor; in almost every case the larger establishments provided the greater number of training opportunities.

Donald D. Dauwalder has recently completed an investigation of industries and schools in the San Fernando Valley, California, relating to the education and required training for technicians and skilled workers.[9] The study is especially valuable because of its comprehensive scope and thoroughness of investigation, and also because of the high concentration of technically oriented, space-age industry found in the Valley. Of the 837 companies surveyed, only 17 had formal training programs offering skill-level or technical training. Nine others made referrals to nearby schools. All but four of the companies involved had more than 500 employees. All companies questioned agreed that there is a need for skilled and technically trained people. Most of the companies, however, indicated they were unable to provide such training and that it must be provided for them by someone else, preferably the schools.

A complete inventory of this nation's sources of education and train-

---

[8] *Manpower Report of the President and A Report on Manpower Requirements, Resources, Utilization, and Training by the United States Department of Labor, Transmitted to the Congress, March 1963* (Washington: Government Printing Office, 1963), p. 197.

[9] Dauwalder, *Education and Training for Technical Occupations* (Los Angeles, Calif.: Los Angeles City Junior College District, 1962). See especially pp. 31–37, 54–62.

ing would, then, give due recognition to the programs of business and industry. A large number of companies have ambitious educational development programs for management and professional-level personnel; many have active safety education and company orientation programs; a lesser number provide organized training opportunities for skilled- and technical-level personnel, and many cooperate with an apprentice program.

But the limitations on this source of training and education are obvious. They exist, of course, only for those *already* employed. Among the employed group, opportunity may frequently not exist because of employment in a smaller firm, which typically cannot afford a program and would not have the facilities or expertise to run it properly in any case. Among larger firms generally, opportunity is limited to upper-echelon personnel, not including those on the skilled-technical levels. When skilled- or technical-level training is given, it usually involves highly specialized training related more to immediate job functions rather than to development of over-all occupational competence of individuals. Industry training is narrow training, the type most susceptible to technological obsolescence. And, important to educational purposes, most of the activities that may be attributed to business and industry are far removed from the problems of youth and work and adult unemployment and underemployment as discussed in this report.

APPRENTICESHIP

Apprenticeship programs have long been a basic method of obtaining occupational competence. Apprenticeship involves a formal agreement covering a definite period of time which binds the employer to provide training in return for the work of the apprentice. Most apprenticeships run between two and four years, but some last as long as eight years. In 1934 the Bureau of Apprenticeship was set up in the U.S. Department of Labor to promote these programs. The Bureau now lists some 300 apprenticeable skilled and technical occupations. It attempts to register and keep track of all programs, but by its own estimate the registered programs represent only about a half of all apprenticeships. New registrations have, in fact, fallen sharply over the past ten years, reflecting the long-term decline in this mode of training. In 1950 registrations totaled 230,823 apprentices; in January 1963 there were only 158,616 registered.

Formal apprenticeship programs will provide but a small proportion, at best about 12 percent, of the total skilled manpower needed during the present decade. The Bureau of Labor Statistics estimates that an average of 520,000 skilled workers must be added to the labor force annually through 1970. Yet in 1960 the total number of apprenticeship completions was less than 60,000—leaving a manpower deficit of some 460,000 skilled workers. In fact, it appears today that only one in ten skilled workers will have any contact with apprenticeship programs in learning a skilled trade. The vast majority of skilled manpower must obtain its occupational preparation either on the job or in school.

There are two long-standing factors related to the decrease in the apprenticeship programs: restrictive union practices and resistance of employers unwilling to bear the training costs. Mary Conway Kohler speaks of the problem as follows:

> I need not tell you the present attitude of unions. Apprentice training can begin at eighteen. But in practice, most apprentices start much later. The average age is twenty-four. And the nepotism that prevails in unions precludes any significant number of youth from getting their training through apprenticeship. Here again most youthful workers are excluded.[10]

Aside from these factors (and they have existed for decades), the often lengthy period of indenture runs counter to the grain of independence in contemporary youth and there is the suspicion that the training and economics of the program leave something to be desired. Apprenticeship in this country is increasingly incongruous. The whole program is long overdue for a thorough evaluation and overhaul.

ON-THE-JOB TRAINING

On-the-job training as used here refers to a formal training program in industry through which the inexperienced worker gains the know-how of an experienced worker. A major part of the training is given at the work station, though this is, in better programs, complemented by classroom instruction.

[10] Kohler, *Excluded Youth: Idle or Trained?* (Washington: Washington Center for Metropolitan Studies, June 1962), p. 3.

Using these criteria, the Dauwalder survey of San Fernando Valley industry attempted to determine the extent of on-the-job programs. Of the 837 companies surveyed, 311 indicated they were conducting such training. A review of the effort of these companies, however, showed that in most cases the on-the-job training consisted of little more than availability of supervision, none of which could honestly be said to amount to an availability of training. Only 44 programs could be found which were on a formal basis or which were designed to provide some training beyond the trial and error method.[11]

The comments made about business and industry programs in general apply to this particular type of training. On-the-job training is a valuable source of skill upgrading for some workers, but has little relevance as an over-all solution to the problems of vocational and technical education considered in this report.

PROPRIETARY SCHOOLS

Post-high-school occupational education is provided by many proprietary schools offering vocational and technical education to thousands of youth and adults.

Many individuals gain occupational skills through correspondence work offered by proprietary schools. In 1962 the National Home Study Council, representing 59 of the larger proprietary schools offering programs of correspondence course work, conducted a survey of correspondence work in the United States.[12] Replies were received from 919 institutions, who reported a total of 3,411,742 persons enrolled in 9,067 courses of correspondence study. Among the kinds of courses were secretarial training, high school and college academic subjects, Bible study, radio-TV repair, and a variety of vocational and technical offerings.

According to the United States Chamber of Commerce, more than 7,000 (including 290 of the largest) business firms use correspondence education or carry out all their training through correspondence.[13]

---

[11] Dauwalder, *Education and Training for Technical Occupations,* pp. 56–57.
[12] *National Home Study Council News,* XI, No. 5 (May 1963), 6–7.
[13] "Accredited Correspondence Education: An Answer to Training Needs of Business," Special Supplement to *Washington Report,* Chamber of Commerce of the United States, Nov. 30, 1962, p. 2.

BUSINESS SCHOOLS

The business school specializes in post-high-school education and training for a wide range of office occupations. Included in this category are schools ranging from four-year, degree-granting business colleges to small schools that turn out typists in a matter of weeks. Many of the established schools belong to the United Business Schools Association, whose membership now includes some 500 schools offering programs one year or more in length. Beyond these, however, there remains a proliferation of other private business schools, thriving on the demand for competent office help. One estimate suggests there are 600,000 people enrolled in proprietary schools, 200,000 of whom are awarded a diploma or other certificate each year.[14]

These schools are operating in a seller's market. The fly-by-night stigma of the postwar years has faded, and public and commercial acceptance is quite good. Some 200 schools are now accredited by the Office of Education–recognized Accrediting Commission for Business Schools, begun a dozen years ago to restore some order to the postwar shambles. Demand for the students of these schools is high, so much so that the schools have difficulty in keeping their students from accepting job offers before graduation. All of them, of course, charge tuition, ranging from about $200 for a three-month secretarial course to $600–$900 per year in the business colleges. General education subjects are rarely taught in programs less than a year in length; longer programs usually include some English, and often some business-oriented economics and psychology.

Several comments are appropriate. The independent business schools have a narrowly defined purpose, and many of them, particularly the larger ones, function well within it. There are, in fact, more good schools in this field than is generally appreciated. They suffer the educational limitations of all single-purpose institutions. Their tuition puts them beyond the reach of many students. In many geographical areas there are no good schools of this type. The work of the schools ofttimes fills a vacuum left by inadequate high school and junior college programs. There is relatively little articulation between business and other proprietary

[14] H. D. Hopkins, "Adult Education Through Proprietary Schools," *Handbook of Adult Education in the United States* (Chicago: Adult Education Association of the U.S.A., 1960), p. 341.

schools and the mainstream of education. Finally, there is a student and labor market potential that urges for expansion in the field of business education.

ORGANIZED LABOR

Some mention should be made of the role of organized labor. Any work a union does in the field of occupational education is directed to its own membership, and, therefore, has little relationship to the occupational education needs of either the three-quarters of the labor force that is unorganized or unemployed adults and job-seeking youth. On the other hand, labor encompasses many of the occupations that have proved most susceptible to automation, a factor that adds significance to any union education effort.

Unions have always been lukewarm toward vocational and technical education in the schools. Samuel Gompers held it suspect, and from his day to the present union support for school programs has more often than not been absent. The explanation, in part, is that the education and training of potential and of presently employed workers has never been seen as a union responsibility, except through apprenticeship, which is union-controlled. The educational programs that have existed have usually been confined to membership indoctrination and leadership courses for local union leaders.

But signs of change are in the offing. Union leadership is aware of the threat to its membership posed by the new technology and of the crucial role of education in meeting that threat. Currently there are several excellent examples of industry-labor-school cooperative programs, designed to upgrade and update worker skills; at least one large local has established its own school, offering both general and occupational education courses for its membership. The plumbers and electricians unions have been especially active in this respect. Yet the trade union movement still has made no commitment to the continuing occupational education of its membership, a reflection of the lack of consensus about who should bear the responsibility for the educative function in the face of continuing automation—labor, industry, government, the schools, or some combination thereof. Union concern is expressed in the recent comment of Stanley H. Ruttenberg, director of research, AFL-CIO:

"Might unions have programs exclusively for their own members?" and "Might educational programs be under exclusive control of enterprises when only their own workers are involved?" rate the simple answer, "Yes, they already do." General Motors retrains 7,200 employees a year. IBM retrains 100,000 workers in other companies. The Plumbers' Union has conducted programs, as have other unions. But in terms of a useful implication of automation for education, the answer is clearly, "No," because the scope of the problem is larger than what companies and unions can do. This is a national problem that requires the cooperation of every level of government and every private group in the country. The job of America's education is to take a look not at one fragment of the problem, but at the total demand that automation has made on our society.[15]

THE ARMED FORCES

Most members of the Armed Forces on active duty are sent to schools in which they receive specialty training that relates to occupations in the civilian work world. The Armed Forces now rely on the "soldier-technician" to a striking degree; they require, for example, twice as many mechanics as they do ground combat specialists, and the number of electronic equipment maintenance technicians now exceeds the number of infantrymen. The Navy and Marine Corps list more than 400 occupational specialties, and the Army lists more than 900, ranging from cooking to radar maintenance.

The Armed Forces encourage all personnel to continue their formal education. The United States Armed Forces Institute (USAFI) and participating colleges and universities enrolled 190,259 in group study programs in 1962; in the same year, 124,337 servicemen took correspondence courses and 14,812 enrolled in civilian colleges. Many of these courses were directly related to the development of occupational competence, although no data are available describing how many enrollees took which courses.

The Armed Forces are giving occupational preparation to thousands of young adults. Since, however, the Armed Forces and the civilian economy both seek similarly trained manpower and since military and civilian training institutions overlap in their work, a question arises whether some

---

[15] Ruttenberg, "Educational Implications of Automation as Seen by a Trade Union Officer," in *Automation and the Challenge to Education,* ed. Luther H. Evans and George E. Arnstein (Washington: National Education Association, 1962), p. 82.

coordination between the two would not promote the interests of both. To date this has not occurred.

Servicemen have the possibility of obtaining recognition for learning achieved during their period of service and thus of advancing themselves vocationally and educationally. The Commission on Accreditation of Service Experiences of the American Council on Education evaluates formal military training programs and recommends to civilian educational institutions specific amounts of academic credit which they may properly give (if it is their policy to grant such credit) at the baccalaureate, terminal junior college, and high school levels. Today most institutions award recognition for such learning. Thus a member of the Armed Forces enrolled as a student in a service school for medical technology might later be granted credit when he returned to a similar program at a civilian institution. Yet another student seeking admission to that same civilian institution would seldom find it possible to gain academic credit for his knowledge of medical technology gained on the job or in another civilian institution.

The contribution of the Armed Forces to the occupational competency of the work force cannot be fully and accurately assessed. This source of training is, of course, available almost exclusively to male youth and thus lends no assistance to large segments of the population in need of occupational education. Too, the Armed Forces have become increasingly selective so that large numbers of young men do not serve. Of those who enter and receive training, many are assigned to "lowest common denominator" classes that lack breadth and vigor, often a preparation of marginal value in the civilian labor market. On the other hand many other servicemen receive intensive training; these people the services make greater efforts to retain. Some 10,000 technicians a year enter the labor market with an Armed Forces technical program background; but valuable as these men are in the labor force, in most cases their preparation does not equal that of the graduate of a civilian technical program.

The Armed Forces are a significant source of technical occupational training. Nonetheless, as the Armed Forces become more dependent on careerists, they will become a diminishing source of skills for the economy, and at the same time will offer training opportunities to a relatively smaller percentage of the growing number of young men leaving school each year. Much remains to be done to ensure that Armed

Forces education is better used in civilian life; that experience, research, and knowledge is shared between Armed Forces and civilian institutions working in the same fields; and that joint efforts are made to serve the individual, the services, and the nation in the development of occupational competencies.

5. The Federal Government and Vocational and Technical Education

THE FEDERAL GOVERNMENT HAS A LONG history of involvement in occupational education. Much of that history has been outlined in chapter 2. The present chapter will discuss current Federal programs of vocational and technical education, beginning with a chronological review of legislation now in effect, outlining objectives of that legislation, and concluding with a report on the Vocational Education and Higher Education Facilities Acts of 1963.

THE SMITH-HUGHES ACT

The Smith-Hughes Act is the first of all vocational legislation. Signed by President Wilson in 1917, the act provides for some $7 million to be allotted annually to the states for the promotion of vocational agriculture, trades and industry, and home economics education. The act today provides only a small part of the total Federal funds spent in vocational education; yet its historical and symbolic significance virtually guarantees its continuation. In fact, its major provisions remained untouched by amendment until 1963; its grants are assured to the states "in perpetuity."

The act was passed at a time when the great bulk of American workers were engaged in farming and industrial occupations. Consequently, the money goes (aside from funds for teacher training and administrative services) one-half to programs for those "preparing to enter upon the work of the farm or farm home," the other half for those "preparing to enter upon the work of a trade or industrial pursuit"; 20 percent of the money in the latter category may be used for home economics instruction for those "preparing to enter upon the work of the home." This statutory division of funds into specific occupational categories remains in the law today; however, a 1963 amendment to the act provides for some change in these categorical restrictions.

For various reasons, discussed in chapter 2, the Smith-Hughes Act was tightly written, setting out in detail what state and local authorities could and could not do in setting up federally reimbursed vocational programs. The act itself and the regulations of the U.S. Commissioner of Education are extremely detailed. They touch on such matters as the age and kind of students to be enrolled, the space and equipment to be used, the form and content of the curriculum, the grade and level at which the program is to be conducted, the length of the school year and school week, the qualifications of instructors and administrators, and many other items.[1] Needless to say, vocational programs on the local level tend to be relatively uniform in all parts of the country. Whether this amounts to Federal control is a question of semantics, but vocational education legislation is one of the best examples American education has of the meaning and effect of "categorical aid" from the Federal Government.

Between World Wars I and II three short-term acts were passed by Congress supplementing the Smith-Hughes Act. These acts were drawn along the lines of the Smith-Hughes Act, the one significant change being the addition in 1936 of distributive occupations to the program's area of service. By the end of World War II the Federal Government was putting $20 million into the total program; state and local matching funds added another $35 million.

THE GEORGE-BARDEN ACT

The George-Barden Act of 1946 brought about a further expansion of the program. It authorized the expenditure of some $29 million beyond the perpetual $7 million of the Smith-Hughes Act. George-Barden Act funds were to be spent "for the same purpose and in the same manner" as in the Smith-Hughes Act. Some minor alterations were made in the provisions of the new act, but again vocational agriculture received the top authorization ($10 million), followed by home economics ($8 million), trades and industry ($8 million), and distribu-

---

[1] U.S. Office of Education, *Administration of Vocational Education: Rules and Regulations,* Vocational Education Bulletin No. 1 (Washington: Government Printing Office, 1917; rev. 1958).

tive occupations ($2.5 million). In 1956 the act was amended to add practical nursing ($5 million) and fishery occupations ($375,000) to the list of approved areas of instruction.

As late as 1957, then, the Federal Government was putting only $37 million into a program which had been allowed to remain substantially the same in its four chief aspects during forty years of operation.

1. The program was "of less than college grade." The original intent of the drafters of these laws clearly was to make this a secondary school–level program. All vocational courses had to be "terminal" in nature, and, no matter where taught, credit for them could not be applied toward the baccalaureate degree.

2. The program was heavily weighted toward rural areas. Over 60 percent of the funds were channeled into vocational agriculture (apportioned on the basis of the states' farm population) and home economics (apportioned on the basis of rural population).

3. Funds were made available only to that part of the program that was of "immediate" value to the vocational training of the students. Money could not be used for the capital expenses involved in setting up such a program, nor for the expenses of conducting a well-rounded program of related knowledge and general education.

4. All courses had to be "useful" and "practical." Vocational agriculture students had to participate in at least six months of directed or supervised farming practice, while at least one-half of the instruction time of trades and industry students had to be given to shop work on a useful or productive basis.

In general, the program was weakly supported on the Federal, state, and local level. As to finance, students, teachers, facilities, educational acceptance, industry and labor support, and public understanding, the program left much to be desired.

THE NATIONAL DEFENSE EDUCATION ACT OF 1958

In 1957 came Sputnik. The national spotlight was turned on apparent weaknesses in the educational system and the danger these weaknesses posed to the nation's space and defense effort. The result was the National Defense Education Act of 1958.

With respect to occupational education, two problems in particular caught the attention of many legislators. One was the relatively slow pace of school district consolidation; the many small secondary schools were necessarily restricted in the vocational opportunities they could offer their students. The second was the desperate shortage of technical personnel, particularly in the science and engineering fields. These two needs (vocational facilities and technical manpower) became linked under the national defense banner and evolved as title VIII of the NDEA.

Specifically, title VIII had the purpose of training "highly skilled technicians in recognized occupations requiring scientific knowledge . . . in fields necessary for the national defense." The title of the section, however, was "Area Vocational Education" and the whole of title VIII was placed in the statutes as title III of the George-Barden Act.

A situation of considerable complexity and disagreement ensued. By making title VIII an amendment to the George-Barden Act, the Congress made technical education subject to the vocational education restrictions. In particular, four of these restrictions have proved unsatisfactory to many educators working to prepare highly skilled technicians.

1. *Less-than-college grade.* Since title VIII was made a part of the George-Barden Act, its technical education programs are subject to the less-than-college-grade provision. U.S. Office of Education regulations, however, have made it possible to use title VIII money in the technical education programs of the two-year colleges.

Despite this official definition, however, problems remain. The fact is, definition or no, that the two-year college programs *are* of college grade. And, some would argue, if the purpose of the act is to train *highly skilled* technicians, then by its very nature the program *must* be of *college* grade. Therefore, they would conclude, the act is a contradiction in terms. A good many two-year colleges have, however, swallowed their pride and accepted title VIII money on a less-than-college-grade basis.[2] Others have refused.

2. *Area vocational education programs. Any* public institution willing to (*a*) accept students from areas inadequately served by vocational programs, (*b*) offer a defense-related technical program, (*c*) of less than college grade is eligible for state authorization to receive title VIII

---

[2] Readers of an early draft of this chapter aptly highlighted the issues in their marginal annotations to this sentence. Commented one vocational education official, "They were practical!" A university administrator red-inked, "They were unethical!"

funds. Thus users of title VIII funds include high schools, area vocational schools, junior colleges, four-year colleges, technical institutes, and others.

The result is that the post-high-school work of the area school and the work of the two-year college overlap. The articulation between secondary education and higher education becomes confused. Technical education is linked to vocational education and thereby to the secondary school, and this situation often further distracts the attention of higher education from the responsibilities it must assume for semiprofessional occupational education.

3. *Administration and control.* To many technical educators the administration and control of title VIII is a sensitive subject. They argue that in substance and procedure technical education differs from vocational education, just as both differ from engineering education, for example. The curricula, course content, faculty, and standards of technical education have specific requirements, and therefore, they would add, the administration and control of these programs must be in the hands of people who thoroughly understand the nature of technical education.

This administrative condition is not necessarily assured under the present title VIII. Within the Office of Education the technical education program is administered through the Division of Vocational and Technical Education, not the Division of Higher Education. On the state level the program is usually administered by the state board of vocational education or newly established administrative bodies created to administer title VIII programs.

Professional engineering societies have been particularly vocal on this point. They insist that technical education is semiprofessional in nature, and must look in the direction of the profession it will serve (engineering), rather than toward the trades or skilled crafts. They argue that neither the number and quality of students amenable to the academic discipline of the technical curriculum nor the number and quality of faculty necessary to teach that curriculum can be attracted to a less-than-college-grade, vocationally oriented institution.

Perhaps the presence, unrealistic to many, of the less-than-college-grade proviso and of vocational education administrative control poses problems more hypothetical than real. Nonetheless, it has tended to distract the attention of higher education from the work that needs to be done in technical education.

4. *Finance.* The one issue that exacerbates each of the three problems discussed above is finance. This is the most telling argument that can be made against tying technical education legislation to the older vocational education legislation. And the financial squeeze facing all institutions of secondary and higher education makes this the issue that cries loudest for resolution.

If the purpose of title VIII is the increased output of "highly skilled technicians necessary for the national defense," one would imagine that funds should be channeled into those geographical areas where a high population density would contain the most prospective students (and where the youth unemployment problem is most acute), or where concentrations of defense-related industries produce a need for these technicians, or where technical education already commands a high degree of institutional interest.

But the financing of title VIII programs is related to none of these factors. It is based on the aggregate allotment a state would receive under the George-Barden vocational legislation: 35 percent is based on a state's relative farm population; 28 percent, on its rural population; 28 percent, on its nonfarm population; and 9 percent, on its total population. This, of course, provides a heavy title VIII financial weighting in favor of states with large rural and farm populations.

This allotment of funds leads to some strange distributions. In 1962, California, for example, which has very high student, industrial, and institutional potential for technical education, received about the same title VIII allotment as Texas. Mississippi's allotment was nearly three times that of Connecticut. Georgia's was a third more than that of Florida. Rhode Island's was smaller than Alaska's. Defense-industry–minded Washington's was less than half of Tennessee's, Oregon's was not much larger than North Dakota's.

Under the law some reallotment of funds takes place, as funds not needed in some states are apportioned among the states that can use them. Thus the above percentage allotments do not necessarily represent what a state may wind up receiving at the end of a fiscal year. But the very uncertainty of the reallotment process makes state budget and program planning difficult. And the result of these procedures still leaves many states with a disproportionate share of title VIII funds.

It is less than clear, then, whether title VIII represents a Federal policy adequate either to the need for area vocational education or technical education. However, its passage was an encouraging development in several respects.

The program has graduated a sizable number of new, highly skilled technicians, perhaps 25,000 to 30,000.[3] In addition, it has provided a large number of technicians new opportunities for retraining and updating of their skills.[4]

Initially, states were allowed to use an unrestricted amount of their title VIII allotment for such purposes as conducting surveys and the purchase of new equipment. A great many states did both. Beginning in 1959 and continuing to the present time, a majority of states have made surveys of their present and projected occupational education needs. The past four years have seen a marked improvement in rate of equipment purchase and updating of shop facilities.

The act itself and the studies it prompted have led all but a handful of states to improve their vocational and technical programs: legislation has been passed, and some states have new state-wide plans to assure this kind of educational opportunity to persons in all parts of the state.

The use of administrative machinery already established enabled the program to get off to a fast start. The USOE brought in teachers and administrators experienced in technical education to provide leadership and initiative in the program. From the beginning the USOE has insisted that high standards be maintained in title VIII programs, and has held conferences, prepared curriculum guides, conducted research studies, and provided specialist assistance to the states.

One important outcome has been an increased understanding of technical education. The interest of educators, of industry, and of the public has been quickened in this long-neglected field. There is new interest in the further improvement and extension of technical education and a better understanding of its importance in our developing technological society.

[3] In 1961, 6,434; in 1962, 9,946; 1963 figures are not available at this writing, though an increase over the 1962 figure is likely.

[4] During the 1962–63 school year 103,000 technicians were enrolled in title VIII extension courses. This number is perhaps a sixth of all technicians in the United States, a singular achievement in the realm of adult education.

THE AREA REDEVELOPMENT ACT

Three years after passage of the National Defense Education Act came the realization that the traditional pre-employment and extension programs of vocational and technical education were insufficient to meet the economic challenge of the new technology. This realization led to the passage, in 1961, of the Area Redevelopment Act (ARA) and, in 1962, of the Manpower Development and Training Act (MDTA). Both were enacted under the pressure of mounting technological job dislocation; both relate closely to the national vocational-technical education effort.

For the purposes of this study the ARA is of lesser importance. Among other things it authorizes $4.5 million for the vocational training of unemployed and underemployed persons in designated "redevelopment areas." In its first twenty months of operation the ARA approved projects involving 15,360 trainees. Significantly, it recognizes vocational training as an integral part of the attack on the problems facing distressed areas. The act is of limited importance from the point of view of money appropriated for training purposes, the restriction of funds to designated redevelopment areas only, and the fact that support allowances for trainees may run no more than sixteen weeks.

THE MANPOWER DEVELOPMENT AND TRAINING ACT

The MDTA expands the ARA training concept by recognizing that the training needs of the new technology are nationwide, and not confined to chronically depressed areas. It authorizes the establishment of training programs for unemployed and underemployed persons who cannot obtain full-time jobs with their present skills or who are working below their occupational potential. Subsistence and transportation allowances are made available to trainees. The Departments of Labor and of Health, Education, and Welfare are jointly responsible for administration of the program. During its first year of operation more than 60,000 persons were enrolled in its training programs; the second-year goal, pending sufficient congressional appropriations, is 210,000 persons.

The Federal policy underlying the MDTA is not new. The importance of a national balancing of people and jobs was clearly recognized by the Congress in the Employment Act of 1946, which charged the Federal Government with the responsibility of promoting "maximum employment, production and purchasing power." The MDTA implements this charge with a commitment to improve the quality and adaptability of the labor force. For the first time, then, the national Government's responsibility is clearly established for the full employment of a labor force facing dislocation owing to technological change.

The MDTA, taken by itself, is far from an answer to this nation's problems of man and work, and, indeed, falls short of the stated goals of Federal manpower policy. The reasons are several, and all point to further responsibilities of the educational community for occupational and related general education.

Over the first year of its operation it became increasingly doubtful that the MDTA would ever be able to come to grips with the problem of hard-core unemployment. The principal lack of the hard-core unemployed is educational, and the MDTA was not designed to correct that fundamental flaw. MDTA programs are vocational in nature, and are comprised of short lead time, particularized courses to teach persons the skills needed for jobs actually known to exist. Jobs within this qualification typically require considerable skill development, and since only persons who are able to profit from instruction may be enrolled, the trainees tended to be the unemployed with comparatively high levels of previous education.[5]

This has left many of the hard-core unemployed untouched by the program. Many of these people, reports the Department of Labor, are "illiterate or semi-literate, . . . unable to cope with the manuals and instructions accompanying modern machines and industrial operations; they cannot fill out bills, receipts, or other forms." [6] For example, more than a third of all unemployed persons had not passed beyond the eighth

[5] See Julius Duscha, "House Group Hears Wirtz Urge More Worker Training Aid," *Washington Post,* July 9, 1963. Secretary of Labor Willard Wirtz noted that 44 percent of all unemployed Negroes have no more than an eighth-grade education, but that only 5 percent of the Negroes being trained under the manpower program are in this lowest educational category. In the same article it is recounted that MDTA officials have had to screen eight applications for every one person found qualified for training.

[6] Office of Manpower, Automation, and Training, U.S. Department of Labor, *Report of the Secretary of Labor on Research and Training Activities under the Manpower Development and Training Act* (Washington: Government Printing Office, 1963), p. 58.

grade, but only a tenth of the MDTA trainees had not completed eighth grade. Through 1963, 60 percent of the trainees enrolled had a twelfth-grade education or more; yet in the *entire* labor force only 53.8 percent had that level of education. And only 40 percent of the unemployed, the *real* population from which trainees are drawn, had the twelfth-grade education of these first trainees. After citing these figures Stanford economist William J. Platt states that the MDTA is really "skimming off the most easily trained or retrained" of the unemployed group and that in fact the "supply of those who can quickly benefit by training will be decreasing rapidly. . . ." [7]

In an effort to come to grips with this and other problems apparent in the operation of the MDTA, Congress, in December 1963, enacted several amendments to the original act. The most significant of these would allow the Secretary of Labor to certify individuals for up to twenty weeks' training in "basic education skills" whenever such preparation is necessary for the individual to succeed in a regular occupational course. A second amendment authorizes a limited number of pilot projects to test the effect of labor market mobility on unemployment within designated geographical areas; the Secretary of Labor is authorized to assist skilled workers with the expenses of moving to a part of the country where their skilled is in demand.

A third amendment moves the MDTA squarely into the forefront of this nation's attack on youth unemployment. The original act, conscious of the prerogatives of the public schools and of the vocational education program, was limited to the training of persons who had participated in the labor market for at least three years; no more than 5 percent of the MDTA training allowance money could be spent on out-of-school, out-of-work youth under nineteen. New amendments, however, conscious of the failure of the schools to face up to the problems of youth and work, direct the Secretary of Labor to pay training allowances to persons with but two years of gainful employment experience, to provide special counseling and training programs for youth sixteen years old or older who could not otherwise succeed in the labor market, and finally, to pay

---

[7] Platt, "Remarks on Unemployment and Educational Policy," Paper presented to the Twenty-third National Meeting, Operations Research Society of America, May 27–28, 1963, Cleveland, Ohio (Multilithed), p. 10. Professor Platt's pessimism about the supply of potential trainees is not generally shared, since the present supply of "trainables" has barely been tapped and continued automation keeps placing more and more potentially trainable persons in the eligible pool.

training allowances (up to $20 a week) to youth seventeen years old or older who are high school graduates or who have been out of school for one year and cannot be persuaded to return. Fully 25 percent of the act's training allowance money may be spent for youth under twenty-two.

AFTER THE MDTA

Despite its initial handicaps, the MDTA has proved to be bold and imaginative legislation. It has been well administered by the responsible departments, and its provisions for manpower research and reporting have led to the publication of several outstanding documents by the Department of Labor's Office of Manpower, Automation, and Training. It has brought the problems of man, education, and work to the national attention. And both what it has been able to do and what it has *not* been able to do have pointed to the critical need for a greater occupational orientation within the educational system.

This latter point is strongly underscored by a recent *Economic Report of the President:*

> It would be wrong to think of the problems of structural adaptation of our manpower supply only in terms of re-adapting present members of the labor force to new jobs. Much of the matching of supplies of skills with demand for them must take the form of appropriate education and training of new entrants into the labor force. The importance of this factor becomes readily apparent when we consider that nearly one-third of all workers in our labor force in 1970 will have entered it during the 1960's. . . .[8]

The cumulative effect of all of this has been to bring the greatest amount of attention to vocational and technical education that it has had since the days of World War I. From this attention, there inevitably came reappraisal.

THE PRESIDENT'S PANEL OF CONSULTANTS
ON VOCATIONAL EDUCATION

The starting point of this reappraisal came in President Kennedy's Message to Congress on American Education, February 20, 1961:

[8] *Economic Report of the President,* Transmitted to the Congress, January 1963 (Washington: Government Printing Office, 1963), p. 41.

The National Vocational Education Acts, first enacted by the Congress in 1917 and subsequently amended, have provided a program of training for industry, agriculture, and other occupational areas. The basic purpose of our vocational education effort is sound and sufficiently broad to provide a basis for meeting future needs. However, the technological changes which have occurred in all occupations call for a review and re-evaluation of these acts, with a view toward their modernization.

To that end, I am requesting the Secretary of Health, Education, and Welfare to convene an advisory body drawn from the educational profession, labor, industry, and agriculture, as well as the lay public, together with representatives from the Departments of Agriculture and Labor to be charged with the responsibility of reviewing and evaluating the current National Vocational Education Acts, and making recommendations for improving and redirecting the Program.[9]

After an eight-month delay a Panel of Consultants on Vocational Education was announced, with Chicago school superintendent Benjamin C. Willis as chairman and University of California professor of education J. Chester Swanson as staff director. Twenty-four other panelists were appointed, the majority of whom were vocational educators or people in agriculture, but also including representatives from business, labor, the press, education, and government. The Panel concluded its work in November 1962, and its full report, entitled *Education for a Changing World of Work,* was published the following spring.

The Panel agreed that a greatly increased program of vocational and technical education was needed. It recommended that the present $57 million Federal appropriation be increased seven times, to $400 million. In the place of the occupational categories specified by present statutes the Panel recommended that a new Federal program be directed to five major areas of service:

1. *High school youth.* Present occupational programs should be expanded, and to them should be added wider pre-employment courses in office, distributive, and agricultural occupations. Investment: $200 million.

2. *High school age youth with academic, socioeconomic, or other handicaps.* Individualized programs of instruction and guidance should be set up for such youth. Experimental or pilot projects should receive Federal support. Investment: $10 million.

[9] U.S. Office of Education, *Education for a Changing World of Work* (Washington: Government Printing Office, 1963), p. v.

3. *Post-high-school opportunities.* Federal support should be increased to provide youth and adults with greater opportunities for full-time, post-high-school vocational and technical education. The area schools and specialized vocational schools in large urban centers were singled out for their potential to train highly skilled craftsmen and technicians. Investment: $50 million.

4. *The unemployed or underemployed.* Youth and adults unemployed or at work who need training or retraining to achieve employment stability should have part-time, short-term training courses available. These courses should be available to others needing occupational updating and upgrading. Investment: $100 million.

5. *Services to assure quality.* Funds should be made available to improve teacher competence, instructional materials, occupational counseling, and various forms of research and reporting. Investment: $40 million.

THE VOCATIONAL EDUCATION ACT OF 1963

The year 1963 was the most important in the legislative history of vocational education since 1917. A new Federal-state cooperative program was enacted into law, highlighted by broadened conceptions of education for work and by greatly increased appropriations. The report of the President's Panel was most influential.

In drafting the new legislation, Congress was presented with two widely varying points of view. One contended that all new legislation should be designed along the lines of the Smith-Hughes Act. The other argued that the Smith-Hughes and George-Barden Acts should be repealed to make a fresh start possible. A compromise was effected, under which the Smith-Hughes and George-Barden Acts were amended and left on the books and an entirely new program was created to supplement them.

The amendments to the older acts cut to the heart of the restrictiveness that had made them increasingly out of date. As labor market realities dictate, a state may now transfer Smith-Hughes and George-Barden funds from any of the prescribed categories into any other occupational program. Thus urban states, for example, might redirect their vocational agriculture allotment into badly needed trade or technical programs. At the same time the definitions of the old categories were considerably broadened. Vocational agriculture funds may be used for training in agricultural-related occupations, without the traditional farm practice requirement. Home economics funds may be used for homemaking courses oriented toward employment opportunities. Pre-employment distributive education programs may be set up on a full-time basis. And trades and industry funds may be used to conduct special classes for single-skilled or semiskilled occupations.

These amendments to the Smith-Hughes and George-Barden Acts reflect the all-pervasive sense of the new legislation: to bring vocational education into the closest harmony with labor market realities. The amendments to the older program are designed to make it more flexible. The new program goes even further in this respect: The categorical limitations of the older legislation are deleted entirely. The new funds may be expended for *any* program designed to fit individuals for gainful employment; this embraces all occupations, from the semiskilled to the highly technical. Since the new legislation generally does not allocate funds for specified occupations, age groups, or institutions, the states are left a much wider prerogative in setting up their own programs. A most categorical Federal education measure has been supplemented by a most general one; the intent of Congress was to foster flexibility, adaptability, and experimentation in a vocational education effort geared to technological change.

The new legislation contains several features designed to keep vocational education abreast of labor market realities. It stipulates:

—The designated state board for vocational education must periodically review its use of the Federal money and justify that use in terms of the current and projected manpower needs of the state.

—The state program must be run in cooperation with public employment services.

—An independent advisory committee is established to advise the U.S. Commissioner of Education on the national administration of the program in the light of relating the program to actual training requirements.

—The legislation requires the appointment in 1966 of a national advisory council to make recommendations to Congress for the improvement of the program. Presumably, this would be similar to the work of the President's Panel; it would be reconstituted every five years during the life of the program.

The legislation also seeks to bring vocational preparation to many groups and individuals not served by the present program. As the older legislation was intended to assist farm and rural youth, the newer legislation contains many provisions that will aid youth in urban areas. Among these is aid to instruction in semiskilled occupations; also, the new allocation formulae will at last enable some sizable amounts of Federal money to reach programs in urban areas. Programs will be supported for persons in high school, those out of school and available for full-time study, those unemployed or underemployed, and those with academic or socioeconomic handicaps that prevent them from succeeding in regular vocational education programs. Included in the new legislation is authorization for an experimental four-year program for residential vocational education schools and a student work-study program. These two programs were proposed by President Kennedy as a part of his special civil rights message. It is understood that five of these residential schools will be established, all in urban areas. Authorizations for these two programs total $150 million for the next four years.

Congressional architects of the new legislation also took heed of the Presidential Panel's plea for improving the quality of vocational programs. A state will be required to devote 3 percent of its new allotment to in-service teacher training, program evaluation, special demonstration and experimental programs, development of instructional materials, and state administration leadership. Fully 10 percent of each year's overall appropriation would form a discretionary fund in the hands of the U.S. Commissioner of Education for the support of special research and demonstration projects.

The new legislation contains a strong boost for the expansion of the area school movement. Through fiscal year 1968 a state must spend at least one-third of its new Federal allotment for the construction of such schools or for the operation of area school programs for out-of-school youth and adults.

No new funds were provided specifically for the purpose of expanding programs of technical education, although the present $15 million title VIII authorization is made permanent. It seems likely, however, that far larger sums may eventually reach technical education programs. For one, there is the large amount of money available for area school construction and instruction: if the present patterns of area school curricula continue, many new technical education programs may be launched. Also, the removal of the categorical limitations means that a substantial part of the new Federal funds the state will receive may be allotted to technical programs and that new technical programs may be established without reference to national defense necessity. Finally, 22 percent of the funds in the recently passed Higher Education Facilities Act of 1963 are earmarked for junior colleges and technical institutes; this should lead to an expansion of educational opportunities for high-level technicians within higher education.

As signed by President Johnson, the Vocational Education Act of 1963 contains authorizations of $60 million for fiscal 1964, $118.5 million for fiscal 1965, $177.5 million for fiscal 1966, and $225 million for all following years. State matching of the new funds is not required for fiscal 1964; fifty-fifty matching is required for subsequent years. All of these authorizations are, of course, in addition to those provided in the older legislation. Unlike the allocation formulae in that older legislation, the new act declares that distribution of funds is to be made on the basis of a state's population, with some provision for equalization based on per-capita income.

HIGHER EDUCATION FACILITIES ACT OF 1963

At almost the same time that it passed the vocational education legislation, the Congress enacted the Higher Education Facilities Act of 1963.

The stated purpose of the act is "to assist the nation's institutions of higher education . . . to accommodate mounting student enrollments and to meet demands for skilled technicians and for advanced graduate education." Title I of the HEFA authorizes $230 million for the construction of undergraduate academic facilities, with 22 percent of that sum earmarked for public community colleges, technical institutes, and two-year branch campuses of colleges and universities. This reservation will assure $50.6 million a year for the expansion of both the college-parallel and occupational education phase of the two-year college. Occupational programs, however, are limited to those in science, engineering, and related technologies—an only slightly broader definition of technical education than contemplated by title VIII of the NDEA. The Federal Government will support 40 percent of two-year college development costs, as opposed to 33.3 percent of the costs of all other title I projects.

The HEFA is a most encouraging development for postsecondary technical education and the comprehensive community college. For both, the bill is a special recognition of their importance within higher education and to the nation. This is especially true for technical education; it now enjoys a clear congressional finding that it is a legitimate and necessary part of higher education, a part, in fact, which must now receive a high priority. For subbaccalaureate occupational education, a gap has been crossed.

6. Manpower Needs, Present and Future

ECONOMIC AND POPULATION TRENDS are significant factors in any consideration of present and future demands on the educational system. The present chapter will discuss population growth and mobility, occupational patterns and prospects, and manpower training and utilization as they relate to the educational system.

POPULATION, THE LABOR FORCE, AND MOBILITY

During the 1960's the population of the United States is expected to increase by 28 million, or 15 percent. During the same period the labor force is expected to increase by 13.5 million, or 20 percent.

The additions to the labor force are accounted for chiefly by the large number of young people (sixteen to twenty-four years old) who will seek work during this decade. Eighteen-year-olds in the population, for example, will increase by more than 40 percent in 1963–65 alone, from 2.7 million to 3.8 million. These figures illustrate the magnitude and immediacy of our youth employment problems. It is a "new" problem in terms of numbers.

During the 1950's the number of youth entering and leaving the young worker classification remained relatively stable; by 1960 the total number of young workers in the labor force was only 4 percent greater than it had been in 1950. Between 1960 and 1970, their number will increase by 6.4 million (from 13.8 to 20.2 million, or 46 percent), accounting for nearly half of the total labor force growth during this decade.

The 26 million youth who will be seeking entry into the labor market during this decade are a far greater number than the country has ever had to educate, train, and absorb into employment in any previous ten-year period. Finding employment for young workers—entering at the rate of 50,000 a week—at a time when the new technology is reducing the traditional entry jobs poses grave educational, economic, and

129

social problems, even to a nation as resourceful as the United States.

The population as a whole and the labor force in particular are increasingly mobile in where they live and work, in a manner recalling the movements of the great western migrations and the depression. In a recent year more than 8 million different workers changed jobs. In that same year there were 11.5 million job changes, two-thirds of which were to a completely different industry, one-half to a completely different occupational category. Nearly half of the people in the United States have changed their residence during the last five years, a fifth of them to a different state. The most frequent cause of residence change is employment opportunity, and the states with the greatest number of opening job opportunities, such as Florida and California, have attracted the largest net in-migration.

Different age and occupation groups exhibit different patterns of mobility. Job change among younger workers, for example, is two and a half times more frequent than among older workers. Young workers who have no skill to offer prospective employers, especially those in the unskilled and semiskilled categories, are the most susceptible to layoffs and firing. Many are in "wrong" or frustratingly low-level jobs, and quit for economic and psychological reasons. The scarcity of jobs for untrained young people tends to keep this already high rate from growing higher, for most of them can ill afford to quit a job, no matter how unsatisfactory it may be.

The rate of blue-collar job change is about twice as high as the white-collar rate, even though the blue-collar occupations are not expanding and people in them hesitate to move unless forced. This higher turnover rate is related to the impact of technology on the employment of factory operatives and laborers. And, whereas skilled, technical, managerial, and professional workers typically change jobs in a purposeful advancement to a better position in the same or a closely related field of work, blue-collar workers—as well as younger workers—often shift from one type of job to another.

On the other hand, worker mobility is important to occupational well-being and competence in an economy increasingly subject to technological dislocation. A company moves to a new state; the award of a Government contract causes thousands of jobs to be shifted from one state to another; a new invention wipes out an industry by making it obsolete; whole occupations and job titles are created and abolished—

these and other phenomena mark the extent to which occupational education must prepare people to face change. The labor force needs to maintain a high degree of mobility, ability to move from one place to another, from one job to another. Current rates of occupational and geographic mobility are high, but they are relatively low for the future needs of technology and are misleading as an indication of purpose and direction. The present patterns of job entry and change exhibit lack of direction and purpose, and too often they display elements of chance rather than intelligent decision. They disclose the need for more vocational guidance, oriented toward the world of work, and for occupational preparation in the school to reduce sharply the wasteful months and years of drift that have become common among young unskilled workers.

Educational training, placement, and guidance must be strengthened to facilitate intelligent, efficacious job change.

MANPOWER REQUIREMENTS

The rapid occupational changes the new technology is bringing to employment have been described. A summary is provided by Norman C. Harris of the University of Michigan:

> Professional jobs, making up six percent of the labor force in 1930, will probably constitute 12 percent by 1970. At the other extreme, unskilled, semi-skilled, and service jobs, which together accounted for 56 percent of the labor force in the 1930's, will by 1970 decrease to only 26 percent of the labor force. But the really significant changes in our labor force, and in society in general, have occurred at the level of the semi-professional and technical; the managerial, business, and sales; and the highly skilled jobs. These jobs taken together, will account for over 50 percent of the labor force by 1970.[1]

Manpower shortages in many of the middle-level occupations are already acute, and will worsen. The limits of this report do not permit a thoroughgoing analysis of supply and demand, but a brief description of technical occupations and a fuller examination of one of them— science and engineering—is revealing.

[1] Harris, "The Community Junior College—A Solution to the Skilled Manpower Problem," in *Higher Education in an Age of Revolution,* ed. G. Kerry Smith (Washington: Association for Higher Education, 1962), p. 111.

Technical occupations. "What is a technician?" is a question on which agreement has yet to be reached. One Government definition reads:

> *Technicians*—All persons engaged in work requiring a knowledge of physical, life, engineering, and mathematical sciences comparable to knowledge acquired through technical institute, junior college, or other formal post-high school training, or through equivalent on-the-job training or experience. Some typical job titles are: laboratory assistants, physical aides, and electronic technicians . . . and not men such as machinists and electricians.[2]

This is a limiting definition that identifies certain semiprofessional workers in fields related to science and engineering (fields in which this distinguishable middle-level occupation was first recognized). But our developing technology includes "technical occupations" with such titles as data processor, construction estimator, marketing specialist, technical secretary, illustrator, structural draftsman, production control supervisor, dental assistant, flight engineer, radiation technician, cartographer, technical photographer, color television monitor, practical nurse, food service manager, government safety inspector, and so on. Many of these titles are new, an indication of the tremendous growth of employment opportunities in new technical fields. Indeed, progress into the technological age, accompanied by greater demands on professional people, will emphasize that those in the professions spend too much time doing what someone with a shorter, more specialized education could do just as well.

How many technicians do we have now? The broad range of occupations cited above suggests a figure in the order of 2 or 3 million, although lack of definition precludes an accurate count. We do know that approximately 800,000 technicians, including draftsmen and surveyors, are employed in support of scientists and engineers. About 600,000 of these are working in industry; the others are in government, education, and other employment.

How many additional technicians will be needed in the years ahead? Here again, no precise estimate has been made. The creation and expansion of technical occupations suggests that the demand for technically trained personnel will be high and continually growing.

[2] Bureau of Labor Statistics, *The Long-Range Demand for Scientific and Technical Personnel,* Prepared for the National Science Foundation (Washington: Government Printing Office, 1961), p. 61.

Science and engineering technicians. This presumption is strengthened by studies showing the long-range need for science and engineering technicians. In 1960 the Bureau of Labor Statistics prepared a national survey of engineering, scientific, and technical personnel for the National Science Foundation.[3] Projections were carefully drawn of the number of scientists and engineers who would be employed in 1970; on this basis the number of technicians needed was estimated. Considering many factors, the BLS estimated that during the present decade 67,800 new technicians would be needed per year simply to maintain the *present* ratio (about .7 to 1) of technical to scientific and engineering personnel.

However, many studies indicate that the minimum desirable ratio of technicians to scientists and engineers is 2 to 1, rather than .7 to 1.[4] During some of the space flights from Cape Kennedy, the control center was manned by twenty scientists and engineers and *sixty* technicians, a "growth" industry indication of the potential role of the technician.[5]

To achieve a 2 to 1 ratio among engineering, science, and technician graduates we would have to graduate some 200,000 technicians annually in the years immediately ahead, and this is the technician demand figure adopted by Emerson in his study.[6] More conservative estimates by the Federal Government indicate actual employment opportunities for at least 100,000 additional technicians per year over the next decade.

Over the past few years, about 50,000 people annually have been entering the science- and engineering-related technical occupations.[7] A reasonable estimate is that about half of these were graduates of organized technical curricula within the educational system, and half came from other sources. It is suggested at this point that the technician output from "other sources" cannot be expected to increase and that, in

[3] Bureau of Labor Statistics, *Scientific and Technical Personnel in Industry,* Prepared for the National Science Foundation (Washington: Government Printing Office, 1961).

[4] G. Ross Henninger, *The Technical Institute in America* (New York: McGraw-Hill Book Co., 1959), pp. 130–33.

[5] Harris, "The Community Junior College—A Solution to the Skilled Manpower Problem," p. 11.

[6] Lynn A. Emerson, "Technical Training in the United States," *Education for a Changing World of Work: Report of the Panel of Consultants on Vocational Education,* Appendix I (Washington: Government Printing Office, 1963), p. 36.

[7] Based on comparable surveys made in 1959 and 1960 (*Scientific and Technical Personnel in Industry,* p. 15).

order to meet the minimum goal of 100,000 new technicians a year, the educational system must *triple* its present effort.

What are these "other sources"? There are many ways in which young people may find their way from high school graduation to employment as a technician. The highly skilled craftsman may upgrade himself into a technical position through correspondence or extension work. A few companies have house training programs. Armed services schools offer technical training. Engineering dropouts often find their way into technical positions. Apprenticeship programs are available in a few technical fields. Ham radio and other home hobbies may provide some background leading to technical employment. And a great variety of combinations of these experiences may eventually lead to *technical* employment.[8]

If we estimate that some 25,000 people a year travel these routes into the technical occupations, we should understand also that their number is not likely to grow. The Armed Forces, for example, are making a determined effort to cut down the attrition rate among the servicemen they have trained. The problem of dropouts from engineering curricula is also being attacked. The apprenticeship programs, small enough to begin with, are losing ground steadily. Industry has shown little inclination, nor in many cases does it have the ability, to provide the necessary technical training. Thus, while the very shortage of technical personnel makes it imperative that these avenues to technical employment be kept open, it is fatuous to suggest that, taken together, they can meet the needs for technical manpower in the future. The only hope for providing the quantity of technical manpower needed lies with the educational system.

The problem is not simply one of numbers. It is one of quality. Though unplanned routes may lead to eventual employment designated as "technical," what kind of technicians do these sources produce? Their training in most cases has been narrow and lacking in rigor and their education is marked by large gaps, so that their future productivity and citizenship effectiveness are necessarily limited by the nature of their education. The technical occupations today form a vital and responsible part of science and engineering, and they demand personnel with the

[8] See "How Technicians Get Their Training," in Emerson, "Technical Training in the United States," pp. 37–41.

background and education increasingly possible only through organized technical education curricula within the educational system.

Other middle-level occupations. Undoubtedly the same situation prevails in other semiprofessional, technical, and skilled occupations. For most of these fields the basic information on numbers preparing to enter and through what channels is not available, and for this reason analysis is not possible. The range of occupations on this level is widely diverse, and generalizations become precarious. This much, however, can be said:

▪ By 1970 the technical, highly skilled occupations will account for more than half of all job opportunities.

▪ In numbers, this occupational area is the most significant in employment growth in the economy. It is this area to which young as well as older workers must look for jobs in the expanding economy of the new technology.

▪ Not only do we need more people moving into skilled and technical occupations but the right kind of people: not potential engineers, not potential mechanics, but those whose ability and aptitude suit them best for this level of work. In an economy which allows fewer mistakes and in which an intelligent and systematic matching of our human talents and manpower requirements becomes crucial, the best middle-level manpower must be sought out and developed, be it age twenty-one or fifty-one, white or Negro, male or female, rural or urban, wealthy or poor.

▪ The skill and related knowledge requisites for entry and upgrading in technical occupations, already high, are moving steadily upward. Education that is haphazard will not be good enough.

▪ Training, no matter how thorough, will not be effective enough if it is regarded as something apart from the total education of the individual. The tests that the new technology will put to our traditional institutions require that the education of technical workers be of a depth and breadth appropriate to their crucial work and citizenship roles in the years ahead.

EDUCATION AND MANPOWER

In short, the need in the semiprofessional, technical, and highly skilled occupations is for (1) more people, (2) the right kind of people who are (3) well trained and (4) well educated. Only through education can these ends be accomplished.

Why "only through education"? The answers have already been suggested in this report:

■ **More people are needed in middle-level occupations.** The want ads section of any large newspaper confirms the extent of need. Present sources of supply in these areas, as typified by the science and engineering technologies, are inadequate. Only an organized, sustained effort by educational institutions can meet the demand for more people in these fields.

■ **The right kind of people are needed in middle-level occupations.** There are certain abilities and aptitudes required for success in technical occupations. Since an individual's decisions about education are also decisions that determine future employment, systematic selection and guidance must be available within educational institutions to match the requirements of the occupations and the potential of people to fill them.

■ **Well-trained people are needed in middle-level occupations.** The constant expansion of knowledge and the demands for specialization require thorough, systematic preparation for job entry. What has been evolved over the years for professional education holds equally today for the technical level: no practicable way of acquiring training exists except through organized programs within the educational system.

■ **Well-educated people are needed in middle-level occupations.** The education of people to enter these fields must be concerned with their *minds* as well as with their *skills*. Technical competence is assuredly important, but no more so than competence in general knowledge in the realm of ideas and their application to one's chosen occupation. This is an *educational* concern. Only within an educational setting is there hope that these values will be given proper attention and development.

The evidence on both manpower needs and occupational education opportunities indicates that present programs and efforts do not suffice for the present or the future. While frequently neither available manpower nor future manpower requirements can be precisely quantified, the trend is obvious. No longer can local manpower needs or manpower preparation be considered apart from the national problem. Education and work have become directly related and interdependent on a national scale.

The pressures of the economy and the population necessitate that national education and employment policies go hand in hand, that, as William J. Platt tells us, they "be worked at in a more disciplined and effective way than the nation has been willing to do in the past." [9]

[9] Platt, "Remarks on Unemployment and Educational Policy," Paper presented to the Twenty-third National Meeting, Operations Research Society of America, May 27–28, 1963, Cleveland, Ohio (Multilithed), p. 12.

7. Major Issues in Vocational and Technical Education

THE FORCES OF CHANGE ARE ALTERING long-held American attitudes toward the utilization and conservation of the country's human resources. We are beginning to understand the direct connection between the education of every citizen and our strength as individuals and as a society. We have begun to see the need for a planned relationship between manpower needs and educational programs.

When major national crises have demanded, as in World Wars I and II, the educational community, including higher education, has responded to the need for educating and training highly skilled manpower. Many observers contend that today's problems of youth and work present us with a new "major national crisis"; their evidence is compelling, and on the basis of this evidence important national policy decisions will have to be made in the immediate future. The task of the educational community is to see that the relationships now being established between education and the world of work, particularly as the result of the Vocational Education and Higher Education Facilities Acts of 1963, are more than "marriages of necessity"; they must also be ones of wisdom. Those who formulate policies at the postsecondary level must be aware of several major issues now plaguing vocational and technical education, issues that will demand the understanding and involvement of higher education before they can be satisfactorily resolved.

EDUCATION AND SOCIAL STATUS

Issue Number One:

> **How can vocational and technical education achieve the status and prestige it needs to perform its proper and vital role in a technological society?**

138

The absence of status and prestige for vocational and technical education has its roots in two American values. The first is the traditional ideal of preventing class distinctions within our society. The second is the status of the baccalaureate and advanced degrees as a hallmark of social achievement and distinction.

The key to equality of opportunity was the development of a unique educational system, free and open to all, regardless of station in life. This belief gave rise to an educational program which has, historically, offered essentially the same curriculum to all regardless of ability, background, or aspiration. Climbing the educational ladder grade by grade and course by course could eventually lead to the bachelor's degree, a recognized pinnacle. Those who deviated from this pattern (nurtured by educators as well as the American public) found it difficult to re-enter the competition. Today, less than 20 percent of the entering high school students complete college [1] (and not necessarily the top 20 percent); yet curricula in many high schools are based on the assumption that college graduation is the goal of most students. The underlying assumption appears to be that the highest level of traditional education will result in the highest level of talent development for everyone.

Thus the high school has been made chiefly college preparatory in nature while the junior college has mainly provided college-parallel programs. This is desirable for many students, but the question must be faced concerning how the other 80 percent who do not graduate from college are to obtain the preparation needed for participation in a changing world of work. The best education for some is not the best education for all. Each individual is different, and should have the benefit of an educational program to fit his capacities and develop his full potential. For many young people this will mean occupationally oriented curricula, both within secondary and higher education.

A major difficulty in achieving this goal is the prestige of the baccalaureate degree vis-à-vis vocational or technical competence. The B.A. or B.S. is held out as the goal to almost all students from the day they enter school; thus, the student of average or above intelligence interested in electricity is always encouraged to go to college and become an engineer rather than take a technical program and become an electronics technician. The average student in the tenth grade is encouraged

---

[1] The U.S. Office of Education reports that 1962 baccalaureate degree recipients were 16.9 percent of the 1954 ninth-grade entrants.

to remain in a general or college-preparatory track in the vague hope that he may later want to go to college and some college may admit him. When the first student ends up an engineering dropout statistic and the second a high school graduate without a skill, and when the nation ends up short of electronics technicians and auto mechanics, we still, seemingly, fail to see anything wrong. The whole question of values within education and society was aptly summed up eighteen years ago by a Harvard committee:

> There is need for a more complete democracy . . . not only between student and student, but between subject and subject, and teacher and teacher. . . . The wish to get ahead, parents' desires that their children shall have what they lacked, the vague optimistic belief of many young people that they may go to college and hence might need the preparatory subjects, teachers' better preparation in these subjects, and their naturally greater interests in brighter pupils: all this and simple snobbishness tend to give luster to the academic course and higher status to its teachers. For the same reason, the academic course tends to be crowded with students who do not belong in it, and hence is often diluted. But this is not our main point here; rather it is a strange state of affairs in an industrial democracy when those very subjects are held in disrepute which are at the heart of the national economy and those students by implication condemned who will become its operators.[2]

Vocational and technical education cannot achieve status automatically. Education, government, and society as a whole will have to gain a better understanding of the nature of occupational education and of its value to the individual and the nation before this branch of learning can acquire the prestige to enroll the kind and number of students who need it. The lead will have to be taken by education itself, and the first step must be the recognition by educators that occupational education is legitimate and necessary education for our time.

SINGLE-PURPOSE VERSUS COMPREHENSIVE INSTITUTIONS

Issue Number Two:

How can general education and occupational education best

[2] Committee on the Objectives of a General Education in a Free Society, *General Education in a Free Society* (Cambridge: Harvard University Press, 1945), p. 27.

join forces for maximum individual development and preparation for work?

Vocational and technical education have been isolated from the mainstream of education by Federal statute, by local and state administration, by professional organizations, and by public preference. The
historical reasons for this situation are discussed in chapter 2. But even
today occupational and general educators are split on proposals to
expand and improve vocational and technical education.

On the one hand are those vocational and technical educators who
argue for the expansion of single-purpose vocational and technical institutions; these institutions are described in chapter 3 of this report.
The position of these educators is that successful vocational and technical education programs involve methods and procedures different from
those of general education, and that as a practical matter the success
of these programs depends on their sympathetic administration by people who thoroughly understand this "fact." Proponents of this view can
point to many examples, historical and current, of occupational programs that have been diluted in comprehensive institutions controlled
by general educators. Within comprehensive institutions, it is pointed
out, occupational programs often suffer in comparison to the attention
given the general academic program.

On the other hand, many educators have backed legislation to support technical education in the comprehensive two-year college. They
have done this on sound educational theory, their arguments involving
concepts of learning and individual development. They declare that the
changing nature of the world of work is such that narrow specialization
leads only to job displacement as the nature of specialties in the work
world is constantly changed by the new technology. In a single-purpose
institution geared to matching people to existing jobs, the temptation
is to emphasize skill training at the expense of the underpinnings of
longer-term occupational and civic competence, related knowledge, and
general education.

Norman Harris, testifying in 1962 before a congressional committee,
stated the problem with respect to technical education:

> Let me call your attention to the considerable amount of related
> technical study. Mathematics and science are the foundations on which
> technical education programs are built.

You will also note the inclusion in these suggested course patterns of significant work in the fields of English, history, economics, and psychology. Work in these subjects, which we sometimes refer to as "general education" or as "common learnings," is absolutely essential to *college-level* education in any field of learning. . . . We should not encourage by federal aid or otherwise, the program of any college or system of colleges whose philosophy is primarily one of training rather than education; whose courses emphasize hardware, and minimize ideas.[3]

By no means do vocational educators ignore these points. Lowell A. Burkett, assistant executive secretary of the A.V.A., has related these problems of educational theory and program control:

Inasmuch as public educators have not been totally active in supporting the vocational program, other forces of our society have necessarily moved in to fill the void. But, if such movements succeed in removing from the public schools the responsibility for providing vocational training, generations to come will suffer an irretrievable loss. Instead of enjoying the rich advantages of preparation for rewarding and productive living, there is the great risk that they will have only routine training for routine jobs . . . that our society may lose the democratic qualities that have made it great.[4]

John Dale Russell, former Assistant Commissioner for Higher Education in the U.S. Office of Education, writing in 1938, declared "the fact that general and vocational education should not and cannot be separated in an effective program for the individual child inevitably means that the agency responsible for the conduct of one must also conduct the other phase of educational service.[5]

The separate but equal approach to vocational and technical education is, in the judgment of this report, bad theory and bad practice. Its apartness has tended to identify it as a second-class kind of education in the public mind; if it is not respectable in the educational community, how can parents advocate it for *their* children? At the same time, its apartness has too frequently led it to be bypassed in the ferment over

[3] Harris, "Testimony on the Technical Education Act of 1962" (H.R. 10396), on behalf of the American Council on Education.

[4] Burkett, "Critical Issues in Vocational Education," in *Vocational Education for Rural America,* ed. Gordon S. Swanson (Washington: Department of Rural Education, 1960), p. 301.

[5] Russell, *Vocational Education,* President's Advisory Committee on Education, Staff Study No. 8 (Washington: Government Printing Office, 1938), p. 176.

educational goals, methods, and standards, and has robbed it of valuable criticism and fresh ideas.

It is high time that the two conflicting approaches to occupational education be resolved. The present pressing problems of unemployment and shortages of technicians are pushing for an educational policy decision that will allow vocational and technical education to develop rapidly within the most effective educational framework. The changing nature of the work world raises the question whether isolation of occupational education will meet the needs of individuals in a technological world. Separation has developed mainly because general education has refused to be involved. It will be tragic for the nation if higher education fails to concern itself with this issue.

LEARNING AND EDUCATION

Issue Number Three:

How can learning, regardless of how or where achieved, be given equivalent educational credit?

Learning is the goal of education. Educators have tended, however, to be much more willing to give recognition to learning gained in certain courses and schools than learning from other sources. A system of transferring education credits from school to school and level to level has been developed, but no plan has been devised to accept learning regardless of where or how it has been obtained. In fact, educators have more often than not been intransigent about recognizing that individuals may learn by other than pre-approved, formally organized educational programs.

The difficulty begins in the high school. Students with little desire or ability to go to college are urged not to take vocational courses because they are not the approved prerequisites and college admission may, therefore, become difficult should they later change their minds. The same is true of students entering junior colleges: only the transfer curriculum smooths the way toward getting into a four-year college. By electing a vocational or technical course, the student often finds a "lose three turns and return to Go" card blocking his re-entry into the academic mainstream.

The issue is one of devising, or agreeing to develop, procedures whereby learning gained outside formal academic programs can be evaluated and credited toward post-high-school study. The problem is particularly acute in vocational and technical education. Methods must be devised to allow credit for learning in occupational programs for entry and advanced placement in general academic programs. Until this is accomplished, occupational programs will continue to carry the stigma of being dead end. Possibly, by giving recognition to individual learning, as well as to the accumulation of time and credits, a change in the public attitude toward, and awareness of, the value of learning would take place. Correspondence work, individual reading, adult education classes, on-the-job learning, and all other kinds of intellectual activities would become more valued in the public mind if they were more valued by the "fashion makers," this nation's colleges and universities. John Gardner succinctly phrased this point in his essay in *Goals for Americans*:

> If we really believe in individual fulfillment, our concern for education will reach far beyond the formal system. We shall expect people to continue to learn and grow in and out of schools, in every possible circumstance, and at every stage of their lives. . . .
>
> Many people who study outside the formal system do so for reasons having to do with their own fulfillment, and care little for academic credit. Others are concerned only with the immediate acquisition of skills, and credit is irrelevant here too. But many others do wish to obtain academic credit. We shall serve these people far more effectively where we have devised a flexible system of credit by examination. Such a system would assess and certify accomplishment on the basis of present performance. The route that the individual has traveled to achieve competence would not come into question. Such a system would permit many individuals to participate in higher education who now—by the nature of their jobs or other obligations—cannot do so.[6]

Some argue that, instead of adapting procedures of general education to occupational education, the occupational program should be organized so that more of its work would correspond to that done within the educational mainstream and could be evaluated on that basis. This would be a mistake. To make an engineering technology curriculum, for example, more like the first two years of engineering school ignores

---

[6] Gardner, "National Goals in Education," in *Goals for Americans: The Report of the President's Commission on National Goals* (Englewood Cliffs, N.J.: Prentice-Hall, 1960), pp. 94–95.

that the technician performs quite different functions in industry from those of the engineer, and his shorter-term, more specialized and applied education must perforce be quite different also. At the same time this approach tends to dilute job-entry value of occupational curricula, a value that promotes student and industry acceptance. Also it waters down the practical and useful aspects of vocational education, which are necessary to retain the interest of the less academically oriented (or specialty-oriented) student.

It will be tragic if the newer technical education programs are structured outside the educational mainstream so that able and ambitious individuals cannot receive credit for knowledge acquired in occupational programs in other degree programs. Credit evaluation and transfer are, therefore, a major issue in the development of post-high-school vocational and technical education.

HIGHER EDUCATION FOR THE AVERAGE STUDENT

Issue Number Four:

How can higher education provide the diversity and comprehensiveness of educational opportunity needed by three-quarters of the nation's youth entering a changing world of work?

In the years immediately ahead at least a quarter of the nation's youth will be needed in occupations for which a baccalaureate (or higher) degree is necessary and proper preparation. During the same period at least half of the nation's youth must seek employment in occupations for which one to three years of education and training beyond high school are necessary and proper. The factors in the new technology which have produced these changes have been discussed earlier in this report. The Department of Labor summarizes the causes this way:

- The continuing shift from an agricultural economy to one that is industrial.
- The rapid expansion in research and development activities.
- The tremendously rapid increase in application of technological improvements.
- The increased size and complexity of business organization.

- The widespread growth of record keeping among all types of enterprises.
- The growing need for educational and medical services.[7]

The issue, then, is basically: for what student numbers and abilities will higher education opportunities be made available in the years ahead? LeRoy Collins, president of the National Association of Broadcasters and former governor of Florida, has said:

> The doctrine of universal education below the college level is now an accepted, and generally accomplished, part of American life. We must extend the principle to higher education. The realities of life now demand of us that every American be educated to the fullest if democracy is to survive in this world, just as the realities of Jefferson's time impelled him to advocate the necessity of fostering a public school system if democracy was to survive on this continent. No American should be denied—whatever the reasons—the opportunity to achieve whatever kind of education beyond the high school that will allow for the maximum development of his abilities.[8]

Diversity and comprehensiveness must be key ideas in the development of higher education. The diversity of the educational requirements for participation in a changing world of work and the diversity of abilities, aptitudes, and interests in the students who seek that education must be reflected in a diversity in admissions and retention policies of postsecondary institutions. Not all institutions can establish standard admission requirements based on the desire to enroll some upper fraction of high school graduates. This is not to suggest a lowering of standards in any academic field; it may well be a method for establishing more appropriate entry requirements in the various fields of study. The one-track approach has been only partially successful in getting the best qualified students into higher education. Opportunity for success in higher education in a broader range of studies may well lead to better self-selection and improve the opportunity for guidance and placement into fields of study compatible with individual skills and aspirations. The two-year college can and should be the selecting device for developing talent that would be lost through college dropouts or

[7] U.S. Department of Labor, *Manpower Challenge of the 1960's* (Washington: Government Printing Office, 1961), p. 11.

[8] Collins, "Higher Education in an Age of Revolution," in *Current Issues in Higher Education,* ed. G. Kerry Smith (Washington: Association for Higher Education, 1962), p. 6.

failure to enter any higher education program because of a scarcity of programs of less than four-year degree level.

Comprehensiveness is also an essential element in the development of higher education. When we talk of higher education for, not one quarter, but three quarters of our youth, we are talking about an attempt to squeeze all into the same four-year academic mould. Rather, higher education must be prepared to offer both academic and occupational programs, a good many of them at the less-than-baccalaureate level. Numbers of students, needed facilities, and teacher supply all preclude as foolish any definition of "college" as a four-year or not-at-all affair. And it does not hold that if four years of general studies is the best thing, two years of the same is the next best or only other thing. And again, a comprehensive (general and occupational) program at the start of higher education could provide an alternative to the academic program for many of the students who now crowd it for little more reason than because it is *the* thing to do and there is no acceptable alternative.

There is, in short, a place for the average student, carefully selected and guided, in higher education—a *comprehensive* system of higher education offering a diversity of opportunity to all who can profit by it.

OCCUPATIONAL GUIDANCE, PLACEMENT, AND FOLLOW-UP

Issue Number Five:

> **How can education establish a firm and continuing relationship between its students, its programs, and the world of work?**

Guidance in vocational and technical education is not an issue—the need has already been affirmed—but rather a problem that is manifest when virtually every study of the field decries the wide gap between what is said about guidance and what is done. The nature of the problem was outlined in chapter 1 of this report. The National Manpower Council has sketched it in the following terms:

> Although a youngster often reads about different kinds of work with which he can have no firsthand experience, when he thinks about choosing a field of work he is likely to be most influenced by occupations he has actually encountered. Generally these occupations are

limited to the principal professions and the services and trades he becomes acquainted with in the course of his daily life. Consequently the average youngster becomes familiar with only a tiny fraction of the many different types of work which exist.[9]

The nature of vocational guidance is well described by Willis Dugan as the

> process of helping an individual to understand accurately both himself and the world of work—in particular, the specific educational and job requirements of occupations in which he may be interested and for which he may be qualified. Finally, help is given at the point of entrance into further training or actual placement in the vocational field most appropriate for him. This dynamic and ongoing process of vocational guidance is based on the assumption that an individual actually reaches his ultimate vocational choice, not at any single moment in time, but through a series of experiences and resultant decisions over a period of years.[10]

Effective occupational choice must lie in the values and goals of the individual; a basic element is the linking of present actions to future goals. Ginzberg has identified a long period during which individuals are involved in making tentative choices as stretching from age eleven to eighteen or nineteen—or even beyond.[11] Brookover and Nosow relate the importance of vocational guidance of the individual to its importance to the nation, stating that "most positions in the American occupational system now have some type of educational prerequisites. A major responsibility for the allocation of various persons to the various levels of occupations, therefore, rests on the educational system." [12]

As education more and more becomes the bridge between the individual and his work, vocational guidance and educational guidance become inseparable. And because of the rising level of educational

---

[9] National Manpower Council, *A Policy for Skilled Manpower* (New York: Columbia University Press, 1954), p. 266.

[10] Dugan, "Vocational Guidance—Its Contributions and Opportunities," in *Vocational Education for Rural America*, p. 289.

[11] Eli Ginzberg, *et al., Occupational Choice* (New York: Columbia University Press, 1951).

[12] Wilbur B. Brookover and Sigmund Nosow, "A Sociological Analysis of Vocational Education in the United States," *Education for a Changing World of Work: Report of the Panel of Consultants on Vocational Education*, Appendix III (Washington: Government Printing Office, 1963), p. 40.

requisites for work today, choice of occupation and job entry are frequently delayed so that guidance increasingly becomes the task of higher education. This delay, of course, does not remove the responsibility for guidance from elementary and secondary education, but does point up that college enrollment is not, *per se,* an indicator of sound occupational selection on the part of the student.

The failure of educators to understand the relationship between their work and the future occupational role of their students has inhibited the development of vocational guidance, placement, and follow-up—despite pleas, recommendations, and studies to the contrary. The majority of students in secondary and higher education state their educational goals in terms of occupation. Instead of wringing hands over this nonesthetic bent in American youths, educators should capitalize on the motivation potential it holds to help students select appropriate educational programs and more realistic goals. The failure to do so has too often resulted in misuse of educational facilities and human talent. The large percentage of students enrolled in college-preparatory or transfer programs in high schools and two-year colleges, compared with the small percentage who actually go on to college, is indication that much less has been done than necessary in matching individual education and future occupation.

The contrast between guidance and placement efforts on the professional and graduate levels and what is done on all lower levels is striking. Colleges and universities attempt to place their graduates, especially those on the graduate level, in appropriate positions anywhere in the nation, or even in the world. Graduates are urged to return to the institution for short courses, seminars, and professional meetings. Their credentials are kept on file and updated for future use. But nothing like this occurs between the high school or junior college and its students, even though guidance and placement needs at these levels are more acute and complex than at the professional level.

A crucial factor here is the establishment of an ongoing relationship between the individual and the institution. If continuing education is indeed important, then the basis for such a relationship is proper guidance, placement, and follow-up in the school. When an individual looks back on his schooling and sees that he was herded into a program that had little relation to what he could or could not do well and to what he is presently doing, that he was turned out of school with a lick and a promise but no help in entering the world of work, and that he has never heard from the school since the day he left, he is not predisposed to turn to that school for further education. The lack of educational guidance, placement, and follow-up, particularly at the high school and less-than-baccalaureate levels, establishes a barrier between continuing educational programs and those who need them most. To ask whether graduates or dropouts will need further education and training in the years ahead (and *right now*) is to beg the question. Given present attitudes, what are the chances of getting them to re-enter?

Guidance, placement, and follow-up must become a recognized responsibility of all schools and colleges if education is to achieve its purposes in a technological society. One of the major "uses" of education is in the world of work. Education not put to use has no value.

CONTINUING OCCUPATIONAL EDUCATION

Issue Number Six:

How can higher education change its form, content, and scope to fulfill the continuing occupational education needs of individuals and the nation?

The need for continuing occupational education has already been stressed. Here again there exists a problem only because of the difference between what we say and what we do.

John Gardner provides an excellent framework for this problem with his description of the link between occupational guidance, placement, and follow-up, continuing occupational education, and present modes of operation in education:

> The successful transition of young people from school to job will become easier to accomplish as the artificial wall between the schools and the outer world breaks down. Fortunately the wall has been crumbling for some time, and is certain to disintegrate further. The vast development of industrial, military, and other educational programs outside the formal system is striking evidence of that fact. . . . Also disintegrating is the notion that education is something that goes forward with no interruption until it is capped by some sort of graduation ceremony, whereupon it ends forever. We are coming to recog-

nize that education must be lifelong, that it may be interrupted at many points, and that it may take place in many settings.[13]

But the educational system is not well geared to this broader idea of continuous learning. It emphasizes the concept of full-time education, over a set period of time, with a prescribed program of courses, ending at a set termination date. It is based on the outdated concept that most people can be educated during the period of youth. By contrast, a good vocational or technical education program will have as many (or more) students doing extension work as are doing preparatory work; this goal has already been achieved in many of the existing programs. Those doing extension work are not necessarily day or degree-credit students, nor is their entry marked by prerequisites other than ability to profit from the instruction, nor is the course length necessarily divided into the traditional quarters or semesters—and this flexibility is an important element to their effectiveness.

As more and more occupational education finds its way into higher education, will higher education respond to the need for a vigorous extension program as part of its effort, a program with the flexibility to meet the needs of the people the program must serve? New concepts, attitudes, and patterns of operation will be necessary.

TEACHERS FOR VOCATIONAL AND TECHNICAL EDUCATION

Issue Number Seven:

How can quality vocational and technical education programs be assured unless new programs for teacher preparation are developed by more colleges and universities?

One of the greatest handicaps to the improvement and expansion of vocational and technical education is the desperate shortage of qualified teachers and administrators. Except in vocational agriculture and home economics, there is a noticeable lack of teacher preparation and in-service training programs and also difficulty in recruiting well-educated individuals with competence in a relevant occupational skill. Many

[13] Gardner, "From High School to Job." *1960 Annual Report of the Carnegie Corporation* (New York: The Corporation, 1961), p. 19.

of these difficulties have been outlined at the conclusion of chapter 1.

The kind of teacher preparation program needed for many vocational and technical programs has never been resolved. Competency in the skills being taught is an obvious necessity, but the present emphasis on this alone is inadequate in light of changing occupational concepts involving the application of science, mathematics, related knowledge, and general education. The metes and bounds of teacher preparation for the science and engineering technologies are somewhat better established, but at present only ten states have formal programs in this field. Oklahoma State University and Purdue have been the leaders, with baccalaureate and graduate programs combining professional, technical, and general education. The National Science Foundation has also sponsored programs for upgrading teaching in technical education. Nationally, however, these efforts are so inadequate and lag so far behind present and future needs that a major breakthrough will be necessary.

For too long the educational community has misunderstood the nature of vocational and technical education; there is much more to it than the acquisition of certain skills through the duplication of work activities. Ultimately, vocational and technical education will be as good as those who teach it, and the preparation and continued updating of teachers for it must become the responsibility of the colleges and universities with experience in teacher education and schools and departments in the relevant disciplines. Such teacher preparation programs may involve some new relationships between the institution of higher education and business and industry. It will mean that qualified students will have to be recruited. It will involve a considerable amount of new research into the nature of occupational education and the world of work since, partly because of higher education's neglect, the literature of vocational and technical education is meager and often vapid.

By the same token attention must be given to programs to develop leadership and imaginative administration within vocational and technical education, a field that is largely ignored at present. Assistance in curriculum development is another vital service that higher education must perform; the new curricula developed at the University of Illinois (on an *inter*departmental basis) for the engineering technology programs of Illinois schools stand as examples of work that needs to be done.

Not all institutions of higher education should undertake programs of vocational and technical education. But many additional colleges and universities must provide the particular services they are qualified to give to this form of instruction. For large numbers of these institutions, the principal service will be a massive effort in the preparation and continuing education of teachers for vocational and technical education.

TECHNOLOGY, PLANNING, AND LEADERSHIP

Issue Number Eight:

How can all levels of education be brought to cooperate and plan the future development of vocational and technical education?

A recurring observation of this report has been the vagueness of the educational response to the challenge of the new technology—or, indeed, the absence of a commitment to make a response. Donald Michael has stated the issue well:

> The problem involves looking ahead five, ten, twenty years to see what are likely to be the occupational and social needs and attitudes of these future periods; planning the intellectual and social education of each age group in the numbers needed, motivating young people to seek . . . certain types of jobs and to adopt the desirable and necessary attitudes; providing enough suitable teachers; being able to alter all of these as the actualities in society and technology indicate. . . .
>
> If we do not find the answers to these questions soon, we will have a population in the next ten to twenty years more and more out of touch with . . . realities, ever more the victims of insecurity on the one hand and ennui on the other, and more and more mismatched to the occupational needs of the day. If we fail to find the answers, we can bumble along, very probably heading into disaster. . . .[14]

Because vocational and technical education are a service so vital to the nation, there now exists something of a national consensus that new efforts be made, that decisions and commitments be reached. The Voca-

[14] Michael, *Cybernation: The Silent Conquest* (Santa Barbara, Calif.: Center for the Study of Democratic Institutions, 1962), pp. 41–42.

tional Education Act of 1963 evidences an administration and congressional determination to come to grips with this nation's problems of youth and work. By its nature, that act was formulated as a bank account for, as a mandate to, American education to provide new and meaningful vocational preparation for this nation's youth. Educational decisions will have to be made, decisions that will affect the future direction of the entire educational system, just as earlier vocational education decisions did in 1862 and 1917. The questions are, therefore, by whom and on what basis.

Hopefully, leadership in making these decisions will come from all segments of the educational community. Up to now, consistent educational leadership has all too frequently been absent. If the educational community does not reach a consensus on how the job is to be done, it may be told what to do through categorical financial aid (as happened under the Smith-Hughes Act), or some governmental agency may be directed to take over the job. Either way, the lesson is an old one: when education has refused or was unable to come to a decision, that decision was made for it by forces outside the educational community.

Time and time again everyone—the educators and the public—have pushed hard toward a new "solution" in education. With the advent of Sputnik in 1957, the public demanded crash programs of mathematics, science, language, and academic courses for the college-bound student. Now the nation has new dangers—youth unemployment and underemployment of major proportions and critical shortages of skilled manpower —and many public figures are demanding that a new approach be taken. Indeed it must, but the present emphasis on vocational and technical education has developed largely *outside* the educational community, and proposals frequently consist of a single plan that will "solve" all the problems of vocational-technical education. In the past, emergency plans have brought both the good and not-so-good to education. As a nation we should have been able to do better. This time we will have to: in the new technology the cost of educational mistakes will be too high.

NATIONAL POLICIES AND OCCUPATIONAL EDUCATION

Issue Number Nine:

> **How can this nation establish coordinated long-range Federal policies consistent with the national need for vocational**

and technical education and national goals in the social and economic spheres?

The broad sweep of national policy exerts a critical influence on the work of American education, and on that of vocational and technical education in particular. Finis E. Engelman, executive secretary emeritus of the American Association of School Administrators, has commented:

> The federal government and its many agencies, such as . . . the National Science Foundation, the Atomic Energy Commission, the National Aeronautics and Space Administration, the Department of State, and the U.S. Office of Education, today influence the educational program to a considerable degree. Some of the effects are good and some are bad. The most serious fault lies in the fact that there is no non-partisan, independent body responsible for developing and maintaining policy and for coordinating the whole federal effort.[15]

Over the years Federal policy has been one of categorical support for the establishment or expansion of given educational programs as the times seemed to necessitate; general aid to education has traditionally been "off limits." The categorical approach has, however, often led to major redirections in the patterns of American education. The Morrill Act of 1862, pushed through Congress in response to the need for engineers and officers to win a war and farmers to produce more food, is an excellent example.

The problem is accentuated in vocational and technical education. These forms of education are closely linked to the economic, military, and social well-being of the country; therefore, Federal programs of assistance should, presumably, be designed to support Federal policy in these broader areas. This is not always the case. The programs of the Department of Defense and the National Aeronautics and Space Administration generate growing demands for technical-level personnel; Federal programs to provide technical education are, by comparison, small. Federal vocational and technical education programs seek to use the educational system as the means to prepare students for job entry; another Federal agency is making plans to provide job training for teen-agers *outside* the educational system. Equal opportunity for occupational education remains a vital and widely accepted national goal;

[15] Engelman, "Crosswinds and Irregular Tides," *School Administrator,* XX (June 1963), 2.

in practice, gross examples of denial of such opportunity occur within the federally supported program. Similarly, Federal policy in such matters as fair employment practices, the awarding of defense contracts, area redevelopment, manpower training, labor-management relations, overseas middle-level manpower development, apprenticeship, youth unemployment, tax policy, and public works can all have a vital effect on the educational system and on vocational and technical education.

The obvious problem is that the Federal Government has no policy regarding the role of vocational and technical education in the resolution of national problems. The effect of Federal action on social, economic, and security issues is to place educational institutions, which are locally controlled, in positions of uncertainty about the long-range policy of the Federal Government. This uncertainty retards educational planning for program, facilities, and staff, and discourages the research and experimentation needed to obtain quality vocational and technical education.

8. Conclusions and Recommendations

A FACADE OF AFFLUENCE AND ABUNDANCE hides the spreading blight of social crisis in America—a crisis compounded by insufficient economic growth, a rising number of unemployed, increasing racial tensions, juvenile delinquency, swelling public welfare rolls, chronically depressed areas, an expanding ratio of youth to total population, and a growing disparity of educational opportunity. At the center of the crisis is a system of education that is failing to prepare individuals for a new world of work in an advanced technological society.

Regardless of his race, intelligence, or place of birth, the human being is the greatest resource any nation can possess. Maximum development of human resources must become a major national objective. The large numbers of youth in schools and colleges represent an opportunity to invest in the only resource which can in the long run bring the promise of a productive and useful life to everyone. Each time this precious resource is wasted, to whatever degree, it represents a grave loss to the nation and the world.

Education for productive work is obviously not the only solution to the socioeconomic problems facing the nation. It is in the schools and colleges, however, that the tragic cycle of low economic growth, unemployment, automation, and inadequate education can best be broken, for it is in the classroom that skills are acquired, the appetite for knowledge is whetted, and hope is kindled. The oft-quoted statement of Alfred North Whitehead made in 1917 seems doubly pertinent today:

> In the conditions of modern life the rule is absolute, the race which does not value trained intelligence is doomed. Not all your heroism, not all your social charm, not all your wit, nor all your victories on land or at sea, can move back the finger of fate. To-day we maintain ourselves. To-morrow science will have moved forward one more step, and there will be no appeal from the judgment which will then be pronounced on the uneducated.[1]

[1] Whitehead, *The Aims of Education and Other Essays* (New York: New American Library, 1949), p. 25.

CONCLUSIONS

This report is presented on the assumption that a too-narrowly conceived educational system must soon be overhauled if the nation is to mount a successful attack on its major economic and social problems. From this study certain basic premises have evolved which are fundamental in considering the role of education in a technological society:

- **Technological change will continue, as a master of all or as a servant for all.** The overriding necessity of our time is to prepare youth and adults to use technological advancement for the benefit of every individual and the strengthening of the total society.

- **Education, although not the sole means, is the best means by which the individual and society can adjust to technological change.** The real task is to make education the driving force in the equipping of all youth and adults to meet the technological explosion already so far advanced.

- **The new technology has removed the margin for educational error.** Historically, the number and kind of jobs available to the uneducated and undereducated permitted schools and colleges a "margin for error" in planning educational programs and providing educational opportunities. Today, however, the inability of a technological society to make full use of uneducated individuals narrows the margin to the point where the repercussions of each educational failure can be felt throughout the entire society.

- **Technological change has immediate impact which is nationwide in scope.** The absence of a national educational policy has tended to obscure this factor, which affects the course of both general and occupational education. The uneducated becomes the unemployed no matter where he resides.

- **Manpower needs in a technological society can be met only through education.** Provision of occupational education as part of a system of postsecondary education, in terms of the economic needs of society, can be equated with the need for general education as a basis for our political system. Elementary and secondary education are universal because they serve the public interest. Occupational education must become universal because it, too, serves the public interest.

■ **Occupational education must become a responsibility of society.** The cost to society of failure to provide occupational education is incalculable, whether viewed in terms of national security, economic growth, or political and social stability. A proper investment in occupational education is at least a generation overdue.

■ **Occupational education must become an integral part of total education.** The importance of general education to the individual and his success in occupational preparation, as well as to the preservation of national values, cannot be overestimated; however, it is not enough for the great majority of youth and adults who work in today's society. To provide general education without occupational education is to ignore the facts of modern technological life; to attempt one without the other is to be totally unrealistic.

■ **Occupational education is the responsibility of every segment of the educational system.** Each segment of education must provide the kind of occupational education most appropriate to students enrolled in that level of the educational system. No single segment of education can provide the diversity of occupational education needed to meet the wide range of occupations or abilities and aspirations among youth and adults of the nation.

■ **Continuing education has become necessary for everyone.** The nation's educational system must develop new ways whereby any individual may obtain additional general education and new occupational skills regardless of previous education or occupational competence.

■ **Higher education has a responsibility to raise the educational level of all American youth.** It is no longer sufficient that junior colleges, colleges, and universities educate the relatively few. Rather, postsecondary education must become a catalyst for the over-all improvement of a free society. The evidence was never clearer that the greatest waste of human talent results not only from a failure to educate the gifted but from neglect of those who make up the great "average" in America.

■ **Sound occupational choice is made in direct proportion to information, guidance, and opportunity available to the individual.** The right to choose an occupation does not assure anyone of a good choice unless there is a basis for judgment. Failure to provide adequate occupational guidance to youth and adults represents still another tragic waste of manpower. For too long, choice of occupation and therefore choice of occupational preparation has been left primarily to chance.

■ **The necessity of occupational education for all could, if present institutions fail in their responsibilities, lead to a separate system of education in the nation.** It is increasingly apparent that occupational education is dependent upon general education; these two aspects of an individual's education should not be separated. However, unless the educational community—and particularly higher education —accepts greater responsibility for vocational and technical education, society will see that another agency does the job. This would be a loss of monumental proportions, not only to existing postsecondary institutions, but to the citizenry whose confidence has brought them to their present privileged position.

RECOMMENDATIONS

The specific recommendations of this study are directed primarily to higher education and its role in vocational and technical education. It is, of course, difficult, if not impossible, to differentiate between educational levels or occupational areas in a rapidly changing technological age. It is hoped, however, that publication of this report will lead to the involvement of the higher education enterprise, including individual junior colleges, colleges, and universities, and their respective faculties, in this field to a much greater degree than has prevailed in the past. The recommendations which follow suggest broad courses of action and present specific proposals for their implementation.

Recommendation Number One:

A continuing national research and planning body should be established with the sole purpose of translating available information into priorities for this nation's vocational and technical education effort.

Data are available today from national, state, and local agencies indicating future trends in occupational change, economic growth, manpower needs, population shifts, and social patterns. However, there is at present no national body whose primary function is to analyze these data in terms of occupational education requirements or priorities. Leadership in the creation of such a continuing study should come from within education.

■ It is recommended that the American Council on Education invite leadership of professionally concerned groups to organize a continuing, independent, nongovernmental research and study agency for vocational and technical education.

■ It is suggested that these professional groups establish a national advisory committee which would act as a board of directors to the staff required. Representation on this national advisory committee should include leaders from business, labor, public schools, the states, junior colleges, four-year colleges, universities, technical institutes, vocational education, professional education, relevant Government agencies, and the general public.

■ The staff should serve primarily as a study and research group, concerning itself with the longer range problems and priorities in occupational education. It should administer no programs, allocate no funds, and have no authority over any aspect of education. The staff should be headed by an individual recognized for his scholarship and broad understanding of all levels of education. It should consist of recognized scholars in the fields of labor, sociology, economics, and secondary, two-year college, college, and university education, and scholars in other areas as research and planning demand. The organization should be directly responsible to the national advisory group which would act as the board of directors.

■ The operational costs should be underwritten by foundation support secured by the organizing educational groups, and by funds from other educational agencies concerned with research and planning in education. This agency should be free, without reservation, to evaluate and propose programs, organization, and future changes for vocational and technical education.

■ Findings and recommendations of the proposed new agency should be widely circulated to local boards, state and national legislative bodies, and educational institutions and organizations. Study and interpretation of national data should result in proposals and suggestions for programs, lead time requirements, changes in educational requirements for various occupations, and statements interpreting national policies affecting future developments in vocational and technical education.

- Adequate funds should be available for such a planning group to secure the advice of consultants in specialized areas of occupational education and other related fields.

- The staff and its board of directors should in no way duplicate or conflict with presently established agencies or advisory groups. Its sole purpose would be to analyze, evaluate, and interpret data gathered by other groups and to conduct research studies for long-range planning. Examples of this kind of study and analysis are to be found in the reports of the Center for the Study of Democratic Institutions, the Brookings Institution, the Upjohn Institute for Employment Research, and the National Planning Association—reports which have dealt with other kinds of broad national issues and problems affecting local, state, and Federal policies.

Recommendation Number Two:

Every state education agency, in cooperation with institutions of higher education, should organize an occupational education planning and study body.

The same kind of study and planning that is required at the national level is necessary in each of the states. Without long-range, cooperative planning involving educators, employers, and legislators, a comprehensive state program is not likely to be achieved. In many states the isolation of occupational education from other educational programs in the state has fragmented the development of comprehensive programs for all people.

- The state planning body should chart occupational education development in terms of local, state, and national manpower needs and patterns. The occupational education planning group should report to the state education department and the state agencies of higher education; its reports should be readily available to the public, the schools, and institutions of higher education.

Recommendation Number Three:

Area conferences should be held throughout the United States to discuss the role of higher education in vocational and technical education, occupational needs of the area, and long-term plans of institutions and states.

There is a dangerous lack of understanding within the educational community and within business and industry of the impact of technological change on education for work. Few chief administrators in school systems and institutions of higher education have concerned themselves with vocational and technical education. There has been little exchange of information or discussion among the administrators at different educational levels, or among employers, government experts, Armed Forces personnel, proprietary school educators, and legislators who are all concerned with the problem of vocational and technical education.

■ The American Council on Education should sponsor area conferences of chief administrators and policy makers in education, commerce, labor, government, and educational governing bodies. Leading universities should be invited to serve as cosponsors and hosts for these conferences.

■ Discussion of this report and the report of the President's Panel of Consultants on Vocational Education could serve as two of the focal points for such conferences.

■ Research by the Department of Labor and the United States Office of Education on the need for trained manpower and the problems of unemployment should be presented by specialists from these agencies and by other experts studying related national problems.

Recommendation Number Four:

Higher education should assume a greater responsibility for the education of youth and adults for occupational competence in the technical and highly skilled occupations at the less-than-baccalaureate level.

Institutions of higher education are yearly graduating fewer than 18,000 engineering and scientific technicians and 34,000 non-engineering related technicians. An effort is needed that will produce four or five times as many technicians as have been prepared annually during the last six years. The chief hope for the provision of this kind of manpower lies primarily with higher education.

■ The board of trustees, the administration, and the faculty of each institution of higher education should evaluate their responsibility for the initiation or expansion of programs of vocational and technical education. The institution's evaluation should consider the following factors:

1. Purpose of the institution.
2. Occupational education needs in the area, state, and nation.
3. The plans of other institutions in the state or area.
4. The availability of related courses to complement vocational or technical education.
5. The patterns of occupational choice within the student body and of potential students.
6. The dropout pattern of the institution.
7. The response of area industry, business, government, and other employers.
8. Possible financial resources available or to become available.
9. The attitude of faculty and administration regarding occupational education.

■ The American Council on Education should establish a standing committee on vocational and technical education. Staff support should be available to work with the committee to keep higher education informed on developments in the field.

■ The United States Office of Education, in cooperation with the relevant professional organizations, should develop definite guidelines for the establishment of vocational and technical education programs. Case studies of programs already in operation and models for the establishment of new programs should be prepared and distributed to all interested institutions.

■ The American Council on Education should encourage professional associations concerned with higher education to discuss the need for occupational education in the highly skilled and technical fields, and the responsibility of higher education to provide such programs.

■ The problem of prestige and status for occupational education, particularly vocational and technical education, has long been a matter of concern to the institutions offering such programs. Recognition by professional organizations in higher education that occupational education is a legitimate and proper responsibility of higher education would do much to break down such problems.

Recommendation Number Five:

The two-year colleges in America, if they are to assume their proper and effective role in the educational system of the nation, should make vocational and technical education programs a major part of their mission and a fundamental institutional objective.

A key to occupational preparation for tomorrow will be the comprehensive postsecondary educational institution. Reasons for this development are clear: more advanced vocational and technical education courses are needed beyond the high school to meet the educational demands of more sophisticated technologies; many occupational fields are requiring more post-high-school general and related education to complement the more specialized technical training; employers favor the older employee who has had post-high-school occupational training; and adults continuing their education seem to favor the postsecondary institution over the high school. The recent expansion of technical education programs has taken place largely in postsecondary institutions.

■ In those states where the two-year college can provide postsecondary occupational education, the state departments of education and state legislatures should increase state financial support, both for operating funds and capital costs. Where necessary, legislation should provide a larger tax base at the local level for public two-year colleges.

■ Area vocational and technical schools developing in some parts of the country should consider becoming comprehensive, two-year college-level institutions, serving both local high school vocational education needs in certain occupations and the postsecondary technical education needs of youth and adults.

Recommendation Number Six:

Four-year colleges and universities located in areas where a

comprehensive two-year college is not likely to be established should provide postsecondary vocational and technical education. Where feasible, however, they should support the development of two-year colleges which will provide these programs for youth and adults.

Several states have developed systems of post-high-school occupational education operated and administered by colleges and universities. Certain parts of the United States have problems of low population density which make the development of two-year colleges difficult. In addition, some states and sections of the country have historically called on the land-grant colleges and universities and the municipal college or university to provide post-high-school occupational education.

The wide range of educational patterns among the fifty states and the wide variation of conditions within these states make it unlikely that any one pattern will or should develop. However, the need for occupational education programs for youth and adults beyond high school is critical in all states, whatever the local population density or economic base.

■ Administrators, trustees, and faculties of colleges and universities should join with institutions offering occupational education at the less-than-baccalaureate level through area-wide planning, research assistance, faculty loans and exchange, use of facilities, and such other efforts as will assist in the development of postsecondary programs of vocational and technical education.

■ Leadership and specialist assistance from the various divisions of the college or university should be available to aid the establishment of new, comprehensive, two-year institutions.

■ Joint planning between the divisions of colleges and universities preparing people in the professional fields and post-high-school institutions preparing technical and semiprofessional personnel should become commonplace.

Recommendation Number Seven:

High schools should establish vocational education programs which offer all youth leaving high school marketable occupa-

tional skills or preparation for further occupational education.

For the majority of youth, the high school experience is the basis for entry into the work world. A massive increase in vocational education in the high schools of the nation is necessary. The efforts thus far, which find only 5 percent of the high school graduates completing a vocational program, are completely inadequate. While the need for post-high-school occupational education is obvious, this study has also indicated that needs for vocational education in the high schools are equally great. The need to combat the dropout problems, the lack of work skills manifested by thousands of adults, and the need for more general education for all occupations combine to underscore the high schools' important role in today's technological society.

While this study is not directly concerned with secondary education, it is obvious that postsecondary institutions can be no stronger than those at the elementary and secondary levels, where the educational foundation is laid. The successful development of educational programs at the lower educational levels must, therefore, become of greater concern to higher education. There is a crying need for greater understanding of the problems of secondary education on the part of the higher education community.

- Programs preparing youth to continue vocational and technical education after high school graduation should be of the same quality and availability as the college-preparatory curricula now available.

- Vocational education should be available for students whose special needs require entry job skills for immediate job placement in work requiring the application of simple, specific knowledge.

- A greatly increased work-study program should be developed for many students who need work experience and job satisfaction to continue their high school education.

- The use of high school plant and facilities during the vacation periods could be one way of starting occupational programs for dropouts, undereducated youth, and adults.

- The high school should assume responsibility for entry job placement and future educational assignment for all youth enrolled in high school, whether they leave school or graduate.

■ The high school should become the community institution providing educational guidance, job placement assistance, and counseling services for all high school age youth in the school district, whether they are in school attendance full time or not.

Recommendation Number Eight:

Continuing occupational education for out-of-school youth and adults should become a major function of many more educational institutions, especially those with programs for highly skilled, technical, and professional occupations.

The American educational system is not organized to meet the continuing education needs of contemporary society. Today, occupational education, increased general education, and related education for out-of-school youth and adults are as important as full-time pre-employment training and education.

Vast numbers of untrained, undereducated, and unemployed persons in the nation are not being reached through present programs of continuing education. To rectify this will require many new programs of continuing education by high schools, two-year colleges, and colleges and universities.

"Public education available to all" has been a cornerstone of the educational policy of the nation. "Continuing education available to all" must now be made an equal part of this nation's educational policy.

■ Administration and faculty of higher education institutions should re-evaluate present criteria for student selection into vocational and technical education programs. Youth and adults now out of school and unable to attend full time should be able to participate in programs for continuing education and occupational upgrading solely on the basis of their ability to profit from such courses.

■ Courses, seminars, conferences, and new approaches to continuing education should be developed at all levels—high school, two-year college, four-year college, and university. Continuing educational opportunities should be available for every individual who is not in school full time.

■ Cooperative work and educational programs, developed jointly by educational institutions and industry, should be greatly expanded.

Recommendation Number Nine:

Occupational education should be an integral and essential part of the total educational system.

Today education must introduce youth to the world of work as well as to the world of ideas, since too few youth have the opportunity to learn about work through experience. The educational preparation of every youth must provide experience and learning that will enable him to move into his next role in life, whether this be further study, either academic or occupational, or direct entry into the work world. The educational system must assume responsibility for every individual's preparation to move on to a next step.

No person can be successful in occupational education unless he has the basic tool skills of reading, writing, listening, and computing. The separation of occupational education from general education at any level increases the possibility of limiting the individual's future development because of lack of related knowledge and general education.

■ Single purpose or special institutions, including the rapidly expanding area vocational schools and the two-year colleges offering only transfer courses, should become comprehensive in nature.

■ The need for continuing education requires that comprehensive institutions provide courses of vocational and technical education, as well as general and related education, for those who are employed full time.

■ The high degree of specialization required in certain occupational areas suggests the designation of certain comprehensive institutions as locations for specialized offerings in certain fields in order to provide the facilities, staff, and students necessary for quality programs.

■ A new understanding of the role of work and education for work is needed by faculty, administration, and leaders in education not involved in occupational education.

Recommendation Number Ten:

The American Council on Education, the American Personnel and Guidance Association, the American Association of Junior Colleges, and other cognate agencies should form a joint committee to secure funds for a study of ways of evaluating knowledge and learning gained outside formal educational programs for the purpose of qualifying individuals to study in formal education programs.

Work experience, individual study, and rapid communication have extended the means by which individuals may gain educational competence. Methods to evaluate an individual's level of educational achievement must be developed so no person will be precluded from appropriate continuing education for failure to meet traditional entry-course or time requirements.

While each educational institution establishes its own basis of selection, there are few tools or agreed-upon bases for evaluating work and other experience for purposes of placing students in appropriate formal programs and courses. There have been successful programs, such as that administered by the American Council on Education's Commission on Accreditation of Service Experiences, which indicate the possibilities for further development.

The development of such accepted evaluative criteria should encourage all persons to obtain more education, and make learning, wherever it occurs, a valuable and recognized asset in our society.

▪ The study should have nationwide support from all levels of education. Procedures and instruments should be developed to enable any educational institution to evaluate any individual's learning as a basis for entry into further educational programs.

▪ In addition, evaluative instruments should be developed which can assess learning in vocational and technical education courses for purposes of applying knowledge gained therein toward additional study in degree and professional programs.

▪ The concept of advanced placement for high school graduates should be expanded to include evaluation which would recommend college credit to any student who meets established criteria for specific courses. The concept should be applicable to all post-high-school educa-tion—general, special, and occupational.

Recommendation Number Eleven:

Tuition charges for vocational and technical education should be kept within a level which will allow youth and adults to enroll on a basis of interest, need, and ability, rather than financial capability.

The greatest selective factor in youth bound for postsecondary edu-cation is economic. Costs of supporting unemployed and unskilled peo-ple, as well as the cost to the nation and to the individual working at a level below capacity, are much greater than the total cost of education itself. Manpower needs of the nation in the highly skilled and technical fields have reached the point where the scarcity of occupational educa-tional programs cannot be tolerated. The need for vocational, technical, and other occupational education cannot be met by private or high-tuition programs.

■ The established practice of financial participation by the Fed-eral Government in programs of vocational, technical, and professional education should be increased to a level which will provide substantial support to schools and institutions offering them.

■ Since the cost of vocational and technical education is relatively great, it cannot be expected that any large increase in the efforts of private institutions offering such programs on a tuition basis can meet the needs for occupational education. Therefore, greater support from public funds is necessary.

■ Programs of grants-in-aid, scholarships, and loans should be available for students electing vocational and technical education on the same basis as for students seeking the baccalaureate degree.

Recommendation Number Twelve:

Colleges and high schools should assume responsibility for educational guidance and job placement for dropouts.

The high school dropout, the high school graduate without occupational skills, and the college dropout have become the major source of two national problems—unemployment and underemployment. Schools and colleges have traditionally accepted responsibility for those students in attendance at their respective institutions, but they have not accepted responsibility for the youth who leaves the full-time educational program. No other social institution has assumed responsibility for these people. If formal continuing education is to be accepted by those in our nation who need it most, a continuing relationship must be established between the school or college and the individual.

■ The United States Office of Education and the Department of Labor should cooperatively develop a program urging all employers to seek and use information from the school or college which the student has left as a basis for employment consideration. A written statement prepared by the institution might include achievements, interests, and successful activities of the student in school or college. A standing invitation to talk to school personnel should be held out to employers. The development and use of such a procedure by educators and employers should lead to a closer working relationship between educational institutions and the world of work, as well as develop a greater student appreciation of education as a means to employment.

■ Institutions of higher education should assume responsibility for the educational reassignment of students who do not achieve the baccalaureate degree. Cooperative programs among the two-year and four-year colleges and universities should be established which would guide students to programs better suited to their ability or aspirations.

■ Periodic follow-up of school and college leavers should become an established function of high schools and colleges. This would form a basis for evaluating the effectiveness of the educational experience and for encouraging educational re-entry for all former students.

Recommendation Number Thirteen:

Occupational guidance and counseling should begin in the intermediate grades and continue through all levels of education.

Freedom to choose one's occupation in a technological society is conditioned by the individual's understanding of the educational requirements demanded by various occupations and the relationship between those requirements and one's interests, abilities, and aptitudes. The changing nature of work means that most young people and adults have too limited a knowledge of occupational opportunities. The development of understanding of one's future occupational role begins at the intermediate grade levels, and it is at that level that the interaction between education and occupation should be presented to the pupil. Occupational guidance and counseling must become a responsibility of elementary, secondary, and higher education. The growing complexity of many occupations and the greater educational requirements for job entry increasingly mean delayed job placement, and therefore occupational guidance becomes a greater responsibility of higher education.

■ Greatly increased local, state, and Federal funds are necessary so that *every* student can receive vocational guidance and counseling for wise occupational choice and educational preparation.

■ Occupational guidance and counseling should be made available to school-leavers on the same basis as to students who continue in school and college.

■ The Office of Education, in cooperation with the Department of Labor, should develop occupational guidance materials appropriate to various age levels which relate each level of education to future work activities in the various occupational fields.

■ Administrators of schools and colleges should take appropriate action to inform faculty members of new developments in the work world, and to obtain faculty discussion and understanding of the new relationship between man, education, and work.

■ Professional preparation of counselors and guidance personnel should include some specific work experience in industry or commerce. In particular this should involve exposure to the problems of employment, placement, and evaluation of personnel in unskilled, skilled, and technical jobs. All guidance personnel should become fully informed of new occupations and of the postsecondary vocational and technical education opportunities appropriate for them.

■ All guidance workers should be required to return regularly to industry and commerce for short periods to update their knowledge and understanding of work changes.

Recommendation Number Fourteen:

Educational institutions from which students enter the work world should provide placement assistance to every student.

The growing national character of job availability in the skilled, technical, and professional fields requires a new approach to job entry. The present pattern of hope and chance does not serve the individual or the nation. Educational institutions preparing people in the professional fields have long accepted job placement responsibilities for their graduates. This same matching of individual qualifications and job opportunities is now necessary over a broader part of the occupational spectrum.

■ The American Personnel and Guidance Association, with the cooperation and financial assistance of the Office of Education, the Department of Labor, and other appropriate agencies, should study the problem of effective entry-job placement for youth. This study could be based on a joint effort of schools, employers, and employment services in a given region. The study should help develop methods for making greater use of the individual's school achievement as a basis for occupational selection and employment.

■ The Department of Labor, in cooperation with the United States Office of Education, should develop additional, up-to-date projections of occupational change in the United States, and relate that change to the requisite educational preparation.

■ High schools, two-year colleges, universities, and state departments of education should encourage employers to make greater use of the placement offices of educational institutions.

Recommendation Number Fifteen:

Colleges and universities presently offering programs in scientific, engineering, health, medical, business, and other fields related to new technologies and with experience in teacher preparation should develop curricula and prepare instructors for vocational and technical education.

Teacher shortages in most fields of vocational and technical education create one of the greatest handicaps to program expansion. Only a handful of institutions have programs to prepare teachers in technical education. Few programs are available to prepare teachers for the skilled trades and industry programs. Too little thought and research have been devoted to the best ways to prepare instructors for emerging occupational fields.

Similarly, new approaches to occupational curricula and instruction must be charted. As an example, a team teaching approach, in which a full-time, university-trained faculty member would complement his own teaching with special instruction by skilled, practicing personnel from industry or commerce, might lead to higher standards of instruction for both the general and special content in the occupational curriculum. The best pattern of instruction for English or biology is not necessarily the best for an engineering technology, and occupational educators should seize every opportunity to innovate and experiment with new modes of program instruction and teacher preparation. Antiquated certification procedures must not stand in the way of any necessary change.

- The recruitment of qualified students to enter programs of instructor preparation for new vocational and technical fields must be given a high priority.

- State departments of education should, in cooperation with colleges and universities, take immediate steps to develop standards for programs of instructor preparation in the vocational and technical fields.

- State departments of education should make additional funds available for in-service workshops, teacher fellowship grants, grants-in-aid, and leaves of absence to vocational and technical education teachers. Cooperative work-study relationships with industry, business, and other agencies should be developed. Additional Federal funds should be available to maintain high standards of teacher competence in the newer technological fields.

- Institutions of higher education preparing teachers for vocational and technical education should cooperate with industry in the development of teacher-training programs. Work-study programs which give both education and occupational experience in the field should be expanded.

- Preparation of administrators for vocational and technical education should be given a high priority.

Bibliography

"Accredited Correspondence Education: An Answer to Training Needs of Business," Special Supplement to *Washington Report*. Washington: Chamber of Commerce of the United States, Nov. 30, 1962.

AMERICAN SOCIETY FOR ENGINEERING EDUCATION. *Characteristics of Excellence in Engineering Technology Education*. Urbana, Ill.: The Society, 1962.

BELL, DANIEL. "The Post-Industrial Society." Prepared for the forum discussion on The Impact of Technological and Social Change. Multilithed. Boston, Mass.: June 1962.

BEMIS, EDWARD W. "Relation of Labor Organizations to the American Boy and to Trade Instruction," *Annals of the American Academy of Political and Social Science*, V (1894–95), 209–41.

BOOKER, EDWARD E. "Survey of General Education in Technical Institutes," *Technical Education News*, Vol. XIV (1954), Special issue.

BROOKOVER, WILBUR B., and NOSOW, SIGMUND. "A Sociological Analysis of Vocational Education in the United States," *Education for a Changing World of Work: Report of the Panel of Consultants on Vocational Education*, Appendix III. OE-80021. Washington: Government Printing Office, 1963.

BRUNNER, KEN AUGUST. "The Training of Subprofessional Personnel in the United States." Paper prepared for the International Conference on Middle Level Manpower, San Juan, Puerto Rico. Mimeographed. Washington: 1962.

BUREAU OF EDUCATIONAL RESEARCH. *Unemployed Out-of-School Youth Survey*. Cleveland, Ohio: Cleveland Public Schools, 1962.

BURKETT, LOWELL A. "Critical Issues in Vocational Education," Gordon S. Swanson (ed.), *Vocational Education for Rural America*. Washington: Department of Rural Education, National Education Association, 1960.

CALIFORNIA STATE DEPARTMENT OF EDUCATION. *A Study of Technical Education in California*, by Herbert S. Wood. Sacramento: The Department, 1959.

———. *Technical Education in California Junior Colleges*. Sacramento: The Department, 1963.

CHASE, EDWARD T. "Learning To Be Unemployable," *Harper's Magazine*, April 1963, pp. 33–40.

――――. "Politics and Technology," *Yale Review*, March 1963.

CLARK, HAROLD F. *Cost and Quality in Public Education*. Syracuse, N.Y.: Syracuse University Press, 1963.

――――, and SLOAN, HAROLD S. *Classrooms in the Factories*. Rutherford, N.J.: Fairleigh Dickinson University, 1958.

COLLINS, LEROY. "Higher Education in an Age of Revolution," G. Kerry Smith (ed.), *Current Issues in Higher Education*. Washington: Association for Higher Education, National Education Association, 1962.

COMMITTEE ON THE OBJECTIVES OF A GENERAL EDUCATION IN A FREE SOCIETY. *General Education in a Free Society*. Cambridge, Mass.: Harvard University Press, 1945.

COMMONWEALTH OF MASSACHUSETTS. *Report of the Commission on Industrial and Technical Education*. Boston: 1906.

Continuing Education for Adults, No. 32. Chicago: Center for the Study of Liberal Education for Adults, March 1963.

CREMIN, LAWRENCE A. *The Transformation of the School*. New York: Alfred A. Knopf, 1961.

CURTI, MERLE. *Social Ideas of American Educators: Report of the American Historical Association Commission on the Social Studies*, Part 10. New York: The Association, 1935.

DAUWALDER, DONALD D. *Education and Training for Technical Occupations, San Fernando Valley, California*. Los Angeles, Calif.: Los Angeles City Junior College District, 1962.

DAVIDSON, JAMES F. "On Furniture, First Jobs and Freedom," *Liberal Education*, XLIX (May 1963), 268–73.

DEAN, ARTHUR A. *A State Policy of Promoting Industrial Education*. Albany, N.Y.: 1910.

DOBBINS, CHARLES G. (ed.). *Higher Education and the Federal Government: Programs and Problems*. Washington: American Council on Education, 1963.

DUBRIDGE, LEE A. "Educational and Social Consequences," John T. Dunlop (ed.), *Automation and Technological Change*. Englewood Cliffs, N.J.: Prentice-Hall, Inc., 1962.

DUGAN, WILLIS E. "Vocational Guidance—Its Contributions and Opportunities," Gordon S. Swanson (ed.), *Vocational Education in Rural America*. Washington: Department of Rural Education, National Education Association, 1960.

Economic Report of the President, Transmitted to the Congress, January 1963. Washington: Government Printing Office, 1963.

EDDY, EDWARD D., JR. *Colleges for Our Land and Time.* New York: Harper & Row, 1956.

EDUCATIONAL POLICIES COMMISSION. *The Central Purpose of American Education.* Washington: National Education Association, 1961.

EMERSON, LYNN A. "Technical Training in the United States," *Education for a Changing World of Work: Report of the Panel of Consultants on Vocational Education,* Appendix I. OE-80021. Washington: Government Printing Office, 1963.

ENGELMAN, FINIS E. "Crosswinds and Irregular Tides," *School Administrator,* Vol. XX, June 1963.

ENGINEERS' COUNCIL FOR PROFESSIONAL DEVELOPMENT. *30th Annual Report for the Year Ending September 30, 1962.* New York: The Council, 1962.

EVANS, LUTHER H., and ARNSTEIN, GEORGE E. (eds.). *Automation and the Challenge to Education.* Washington: National Education Association, 1962.

Facts and Figures on Adult Education, Vol. I (April 1963), No. 1. Washington: Division of Adult Education Service, National Education Association.

GARDNER, JOHN W. "From High School to Job," *1960 Annual Report of the Carnegie Corporation of New York.* New York: The Corporation, 1961.

――――. "National Goals in Education," *Goals for Americans: The Report of the President's Commission on National Goals,* pp. 81–100. Englewood Cliffs, N.J.: Prentice-Hall, Inc., 1960.

GEORGIA STATE BOARD OF VOCATIONAL EDUCATION. *The Challenge of Change for Vocational Education.* Atlanta: State Department of Education, 1962.

GINZBERG, ELI, *et al. Occupational Choice.* New York: Columbia University Press, 1951.

HARRIS, NORMAN C. "The Community Junior College, A Solution to the Skilled Manpower Problem," G. Kerry Smith (ed.), *Higher Education in an Age of Revolution.* Washington: Association for Higher Education, National Education Association, 1962.

――――. "Meeting the Post-High School Educational Needs of the Vast 'Middle Group' of High School Graduates," Presentation to the Committee on Articulation of Schools and Colleges, North Central Association of Colleges and Secondary Schools, Chicago, March 19, 1963.

————. "Testimony on the Technical Education Act of 1962 [H.R. 10396]." Hearings before the Special Subcommittee on Education, House Committee on Education and Labor, June 1, 1962. Multilithed. Washington: American Council on Education, 1962.

HELLER, WALTER W. "Men, Money, and Materials," *Educational Record,* XLIV (January 1963), 12–16.

HENNINGER, G. ROSS. *The Technical Institute in America.* New York: McGraw-Hill Book Co., 1959.

HOPKINS, H. D. "Adult Education Through Proprietary Schools," *Handbook of Adult Education in the United States,* pp. 339–44. Chicago: Adult Education Association of the U.S.A., 1960.

IOWA STATE DEPARTMENT OF PUBLIC INSTRUCTION. *Education Beyond High-School Age, The Community College.* Des Moines: State of Iowa, 1962.

JOHNSTONE, JOHN W. E. *Volunteers for Learning: A Study of the Educational Pursuits of American Adults.* National Opinion Research Center Report No. 89. Chicago: The Center, 1963.

KENTUCKY STATE DEPARTMENT OF EDUCATION. *Vocational, Industrial, and Technical Education.* Frankfort: The Department, n.d.

KOHLER, MARY CONWAY. *Excluded Youth: Idle or Trained?* Washington: Washington Center for Metropolitan Studies Public Service Leaflet. Washington: The Center, 1962.

————. *Youth in the World of Work.* New York: Taconic Foundation, 1962.

LEONARD, GEORGE B. "Are We Cheating Twenty Million Students?" *Look,* June 4, 1963, p. 38.

LEVITAN, SAR A. *Vocational Education and Federal Policy.* Kalamazoo, Mich.: W. E. Upjohn Institute for Employment Research, 1963.

Manpower Report of the President and A Report on Manpower Requirements, Resources, Utilization, and Training by the United States Department of Labor, Transmitted to the Congress, March 1963. Washington: Government Printing Office, 1963.

MCGRATH, EARL JAMES. *Education: The Wellspring of Democracy.* University: University of Alabama Press, 1951.

————. *The Future of the Community College.* Buffalo, N.Y.: School of Education, University of Buffalo, 1962.

————, and RUSSELL, CHARLES H. *Are Liberal Arts Colleges Becoming Professional Schools?* New York: Institute of Higher Education, Teachers College, Columbia University, 1958.

MCLURE, WILLIAM P. "The Challenge of Vocational and Technical Education," *Phi Delta Kappan,* XLIII (February 1962), 212–17.

————. *Vocational and Technical Education in Illinois: Tomorrow's Challenge.* Springfield: Office of the Superintendent of Public Instruction, State of Illinois, 1960.

MAYS, ARTHUR B. "50 Years of Progress in Vocational and Practical Arts Education," *American Vocational Journal*, XXXI (December 1956), 37–38.

MEDSKER, LELAND L. *The Junior College: Progress and Prospect.* New York: McGraw-Hill Book Co., 1960.

MICHAEL, DONALD N. *Cybernation: The Silent Conquest.* Santa Barbara, Calif.: Center for the Study of Democratic Institutions, 1962.

MINER, JERRY. *Social and Economic Factors in Spending for Public Education.* Syracuse, N.Y.: Syracuse University Press, 1963.

MOHS, MILTON C. *Service Through Placement in the Junior College.* Washington: American Association of Junior Colleges, 1962.

MORTON, JOHN R. *University Extension in the United States.* Birmingham: University of Alabama Press, 1953.

MUNGER, FRANK J., and FENNO, RICHARD F., JR. *National Politics and Federal Aid to Education.* Syracuse, N.Y. Syracuse University Press, 1962.

NATIONAL EDUCATION ASSOCIATION. *Journal of Proceedings and Addresses of the 46th Annual Meeting, 1908.* Washington: The Association, 1908. Pp. 155–94.

National Home Study Council News, XI, No. 5 (May 1963), 6–7.

NATIONAL MANPOWER COUNCIL. *A Policy for Skilled Manpower.* New York: Columbia University Press, 1954.

NATIONAL SCIENCE FOUNDATION. *Employment of Scientific and Technical Personnel in State Government Agencies: Report on a 1959 Survey.* NSF 61–17. Washington: Government Printing Office, 1961.

————. *The Long-Range Demand for Scientific and Technical Personnel, A Methodological Study,* Prepared by the Bureau of Labor Statistics, U.S. Department of Labor. NSF 61–65. Washington: Government Printing Office, 1961.

————. *Scientific and Technical Personnel in Industry,* Prepared by the Bureau of Labor Statistics, U.S. Department of Labor. NSF 61–75. Washington: Government Printing Office, 1961.

————. *Scientific and Technical Personnel in the Federal Government 1956 and 1960.* NSF 62–26. Washington: Government Printing Office, 1962.

————. *Scientific Manpower 1960.* NSF 61–34. Washington: Government Printing Office, 1961.

[North Carolina] State Board of Education. *A Guide to the Further Development of Industrial Education Centers in North Carolina.* Raleigh: The Board, 1963.

NORTON, JOHN K. *Changing Demands on Education and Their Fiscal Implications.* Washington: National Committee for Support of the Public Schools, 1963.

OKLAHOMA STATE REGENTS FOR HIGHER EDUCATION. *Self Study of Higher Education in Oklahoma: Organization and Plan,* by John J. Coffelt. Report 1. Oklahoma City: The Regents, 1962.

PENNSYLVANIA, COMMONWEALTH OF. DEPARTMENT OF PUBLIC INSTRUCTION. *Why Pennsylvania Needs Technical and Industrial Education in the 1960's.* Harrisburg, Pa.: The Department, 1961.

PIEL, GERARD. *Consumers of Abundance.* Santa Barbara, Calif.: Center for the Study of Democratic Institutions, 1961.

PLATT, WILLIAM J. "Remarks on Unemployment and Educational Policy." Paper presented to the 23rd National Meeting, Operations Research Society of America, May 27–28, 1963, Cleveland, Ohio. Multilithed.

POST-HIGH SCHOOL EDUCATION STUDY COMMISSION. *Report of the Post-High School Education Study Commission.* Indianapolis, Ind.: The Commission, 1962.

PRESIDENT'S COMMITTEE ON YOUTH EMPLOYMENT. *The Challenge of Jobless Youth.* Washington: Government Printing Office, 1963.

PROSSER, CHARLES A., and ALLEN, CHARLES R. *Vocational Education in a Democracy.* New York: Appleton-Century, 1925.

RESEARCH COUNCIL OF THE GREAT CITIES PROGRAM FOR SCHOOL IMPROVEMENT. *Report Submitted to the Panel of Consultants on Vocational Education in the Large Cities of America.* Mimeographed. Washington: The Council, 1962.

RUSSELL, JAMES E. "The Trend in American Education," *Educational Review,* XXXII (June 1906), 28–41.

RUSSELL, JOHN DALE. *Vocational Education.* President's Advisory Committee on Education, Staff Study No. 8. Washington: Government Printing Office, 1938.

RUTTENBERG, STANLEY H. "Educational Implications of Automation as Seen by a Trade Union Officer," Luther H. Evans and George E. Arnstein (eds.), *Automation and the Challenge to Education.* Washington: National Education Association, 1962.

SERBEIN, OSCAR N. *Educational Activities of Business.* Washington: American Council on Education, 1961.

SEXTON, PATRICIA CAYO. "The Elite and the Mosser: Tug of War in the Schools," *Education Synopsis,* Winter 1963.

SMITH, HAROLD T. *Education and Training for the World of Work: A Vocational Education Program for the State of Michigan.* Kalamazoo, Mich.: W. E. Upjohn Institute for Employment Research, 1963.

SUFRIN, SIDNEY C. *Administering the National Defense Education Act.* Syracuse, N.Y.: Syracuse University Press, 1963.

―――. *Issues in Federal Aid to Education.* Syracuse, N.Y.: Syracuse University Press, 1962.

U.S. CONGRESS. HOUSE OF REPRESENTATIVES. *Report of the Commission on National Aid to Vocational Education.* 63d Cong., 2d Sess., H.R. Doc. 1004. Washington: Government Printing Office, 1914.

U.S. DEPARTMENT OF HEALTH, EDUCATION, AND WELFARE. OFFICE OF EDUCATION. *Administration of Vocational Education: Rules and Regulations.* FS 5.123.1. Rev. ed. Washington: Government Printing Office, 1958.

―――. *Digest of Annual Reports of State Boards of Vocational Education, Fiscal Year Ended June 30, 1962.* OE-80008-62. Washington: Government Printing Office, 1963.

―――. *Economics of Higher Education,* ed. Selma J. Muskin. OE-50027. Washington: Government Printing Office, 1962.

―――. *Education for a Changing World of Work: Report of the Panel of Consultants on Vocational Education.* OE-80021. Washington: Government Printing Office, 1963.

―――. *Land-Grant Colleges and Universities, 1862-1962,* by Henry S. Brunner. OE-50030. Washington: Government Printing Office, 1962.

―――. *Occupational Criteria and Preparatory Curriculum Patterns in Technical Education Programs.* OE-80015. Washington: Government Printing Office, 1962.

―――. *Organized Occupational Curriculums in Higher Education,* by Ken August Brunner and D. Grant Morrison. OE-54012. Washington: Government Printing Office, 1961.

―――. "Progress in Title VIII Programs, Fiscal Year 1962." Mimeographed. Washington: Division of Vocational and Technical Education, The Office, 1963.

―――. *Progress of Public Education in the United States of America, 1961–62.* OE-10005-62-A. Washington: Government Printing Office, 1962.

―――. *Public Vocational Education Programs: Characteristics of Programs under Provisions of the Federal Vocational Education Acts.* OE-80007. Washington: Government Printing Office, 1960.

―――. *Retention and Withdrawal of College Students*, by Robert E. Iffert. FS 5.3:958/1. Washington: Government Printing Office, 1957.

―――. *State Boards Responsible for Higher Education*, by S. V. Martorana and Ernest V. Hollis. OE-53005. Washington: Government Printing Office, 1960.

―――. *Statistics of Public School Adult Education*, by Martha V. Woodward. OE-13009. Washington: Government Printing Office, 1961.

―――. *Total Enrollment in Institutions of Higher Education, First Term, 1959–60*. OE-54025. Washington: Government Printing Office, 1962.

―――. *Trade and Industrial Education for the 1960's*. OE-84001. Washington: Government Printing Office, 1959.

U.S. DEPARTMENT OF LABOR. *Manpower, Challenge of the 1960's*. Washington: Government Printing Office, 1961.

―――. *A Report on Manpower Requirements, Resources, Utilization, and Training*. [See *Manpower Report of the President.* . . .]

―――. BUREAU OF APPRENTICESHIP AND TRAINING. *The National Apprenticeship Program*. Washington: Government Printing Office, 1962.

―――. BUREAU OF THE CENSUS. *Historical Statistics of the United States, Colonial Times to 1957*. Washington: Government Printing Office, 1960.

―――. BUREAU OF LABOR STATISTICS. *From School to Work: The Early Employment Experience in Seven Communities, 1952–1957*. Washington: Government Printing Office, 1961.

―――. BUREAU OF LABOR STATISTICS. *Interim Revised Projections of U.S. Labor Force, 1965–75*. Special Labor Force Report, No. 24. Washington: Government Printing Office, 1962.

―――. OFFICE OF MANPOWER, AUTOMATION, AND TRAINING. *Manpower and Training: Trends, Outlook, Programs*. Washington: Government Printing Office, 1962.

―――. OFFICE OF MANPOWER, AUTOMATION, AND TRAINING. *Report of the Secretary of Labor on Research and Training Activities under the Manpower Development and Training Act*. Washington: Government Printing Office, 1963.

―――. OFFICE OF MANPOWER, AUTOMATION, AND TRAINING. *Young Workers: Their Special Training Needs*. Washington: Government Printing Office, 1963.

Vocationally Talented Pupils: A Report of the Division of Field Studies and Research, Graduate School of Education. New Brunswick, N.J.: Rutgers—The State University, 1962.

WATSON, GOODWIN (ed.). *No Room at the Bottom: Automation and the Reluctant Learner*. Washington: National Education Association, 1963.

WEBER, ROBERT E. "Man and His Environment—1980." Background paper prepared for the annual meeting of the Board of Trustees of the Educational Testing Service, May 1963. Multilithed.

WHITLOCK, JAMES W., and WILLIAMS, BILLY J. *Jobs and Training for Southern Youth.* Nashville, Tenn.: Center for Southern Education Studies, George Peabody College for Teachers, 1963.

WICKENDEN, WILLIAM E. *A Comparative Study of Engineering Education in the United States and in Europe.* Society for the Promotion of Engineering Education, 1929.

[WISCONSIN] STATE BOARD OF VOCATIONAL AND ADULT EDUCATION. *Post-High School Vocational-Technical Education in Wisconsin.* Madison: The State Board, 1962.

"Working for Training," *The Economist* [London], Feb. 9, 1963.

WORLD CONFEDERATION OF ORGANIZATIONS OF THE TEACHING PROFESSION. *Education in a Technical Age: A Study Developed by WCOTP Member Organizations and Presented to the 11th Assembly of Delegates, Stockholm, 1962.* Washington: The Confederation, 1962.

WRENN, C. GILBERT. *The Counselor in a Changing World.* Washington: American Personnel and Guidance Association, 1962.

YOUMANS, E. GRANT. "The Rural School Dropout: A Ten Year Follow-Up Study of Eastern Kentucky Youth," *Bulletin of the Bureau of School Service.* Lexington: College of Education, University of Kentucky, September 1963.

AMERICAN COUNCIL ON EDUCATION

LOGAN WILSON, *President*

The American Council on Education, founded in 1918, is a council of educational organizations and institutions. Its purpose is to advance education and educational methods through comprehensive voluntary and cooperative action on the part of American educational associations, organizations, and institutions.